Toilets of the WORLD

GEOF PRIGGE

NEW HOLLAND

INTRODUCTION

Toilets of the WORLD

Going to the toilet in some countries can be a mammoth undertaking. Finding a toilet is sometimes the hardest part. What greets you more often than not when you push open the door (if there is a door) can be absolutely nightmarish. Clean porcelain and polished tiles are far from the reality of many third world lavatories. What follows is a wide selection of the world's dunnies, from sea level to the top of the world, shocking, colourful, funny dunnies—they're all here. Toilets in Tibet, potties in Poland, lavatories in Latvia, shithouses in Siberia and lots more—even Aussie dunnies. Shot predominantly by me but with the help of some of my friends, my collection of loos (in alphabetical order) shows a wide selection of where to go and where not to go when nature calls. You, the reader, can make up your own mind as to which is which.

Geof Prigge

ACKNOWLEDGEMENTS

My thanks go to Dave MacDonald of Scotland and Frank Voellm from Schwieberdingen, Germany, both of whom I met during my Nepal–Tibet travels in 2004. Their photographic input allowed me to portray areas I haven't visited like Siberia and Mt Sinai.

Austria—Vienna

Public toilet designed by Hundertwasser (born Friedrich Stowasser, 1928–2000). As an artist, architect and philosopher he liked to break the rules of conventional architecture. His most famous works are in Europe—Kunst Haus Wien (Vienna); the Church of St Barbara in Bärnbach; The Motorway Restaurant in Bad Fischau; The District Heating Plant in Spittelau, Vienna; and his 'in the meadows' Housing Complex in Taunus. His vegetative paintings, as he referred to them, are equally unique. He also designed public toilets in Europe and New Zealand.

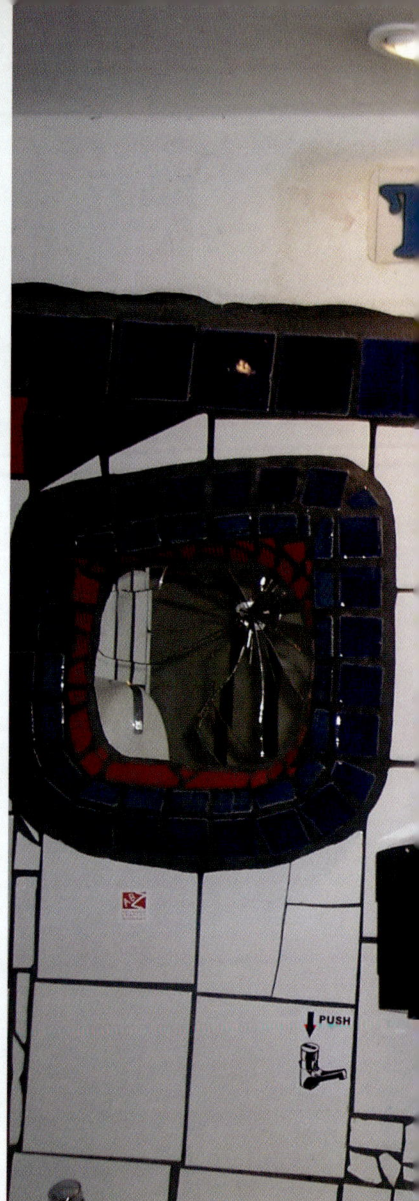

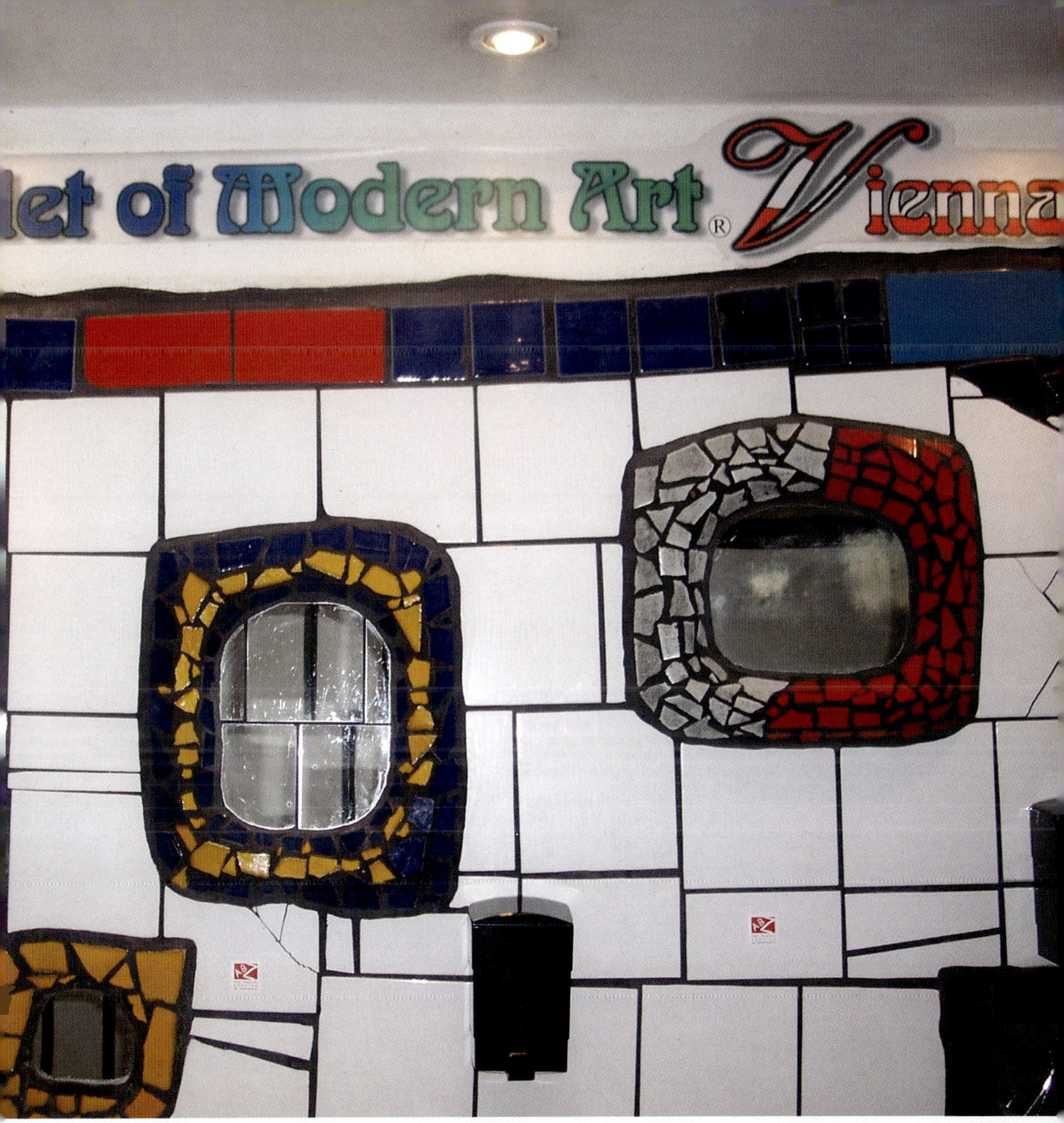
let of Modern Art® Vienna

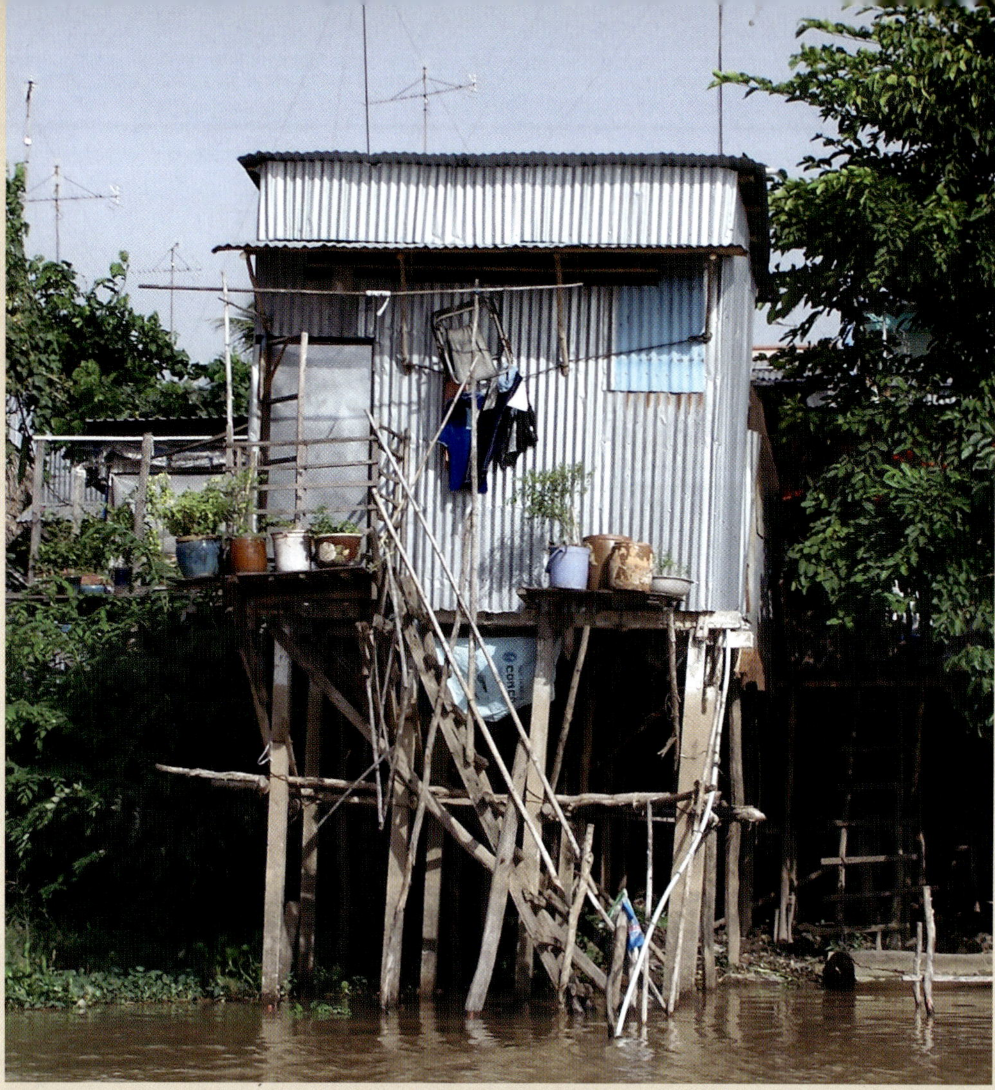

Cambodia—Mekong Delta
Which part's the toilet?

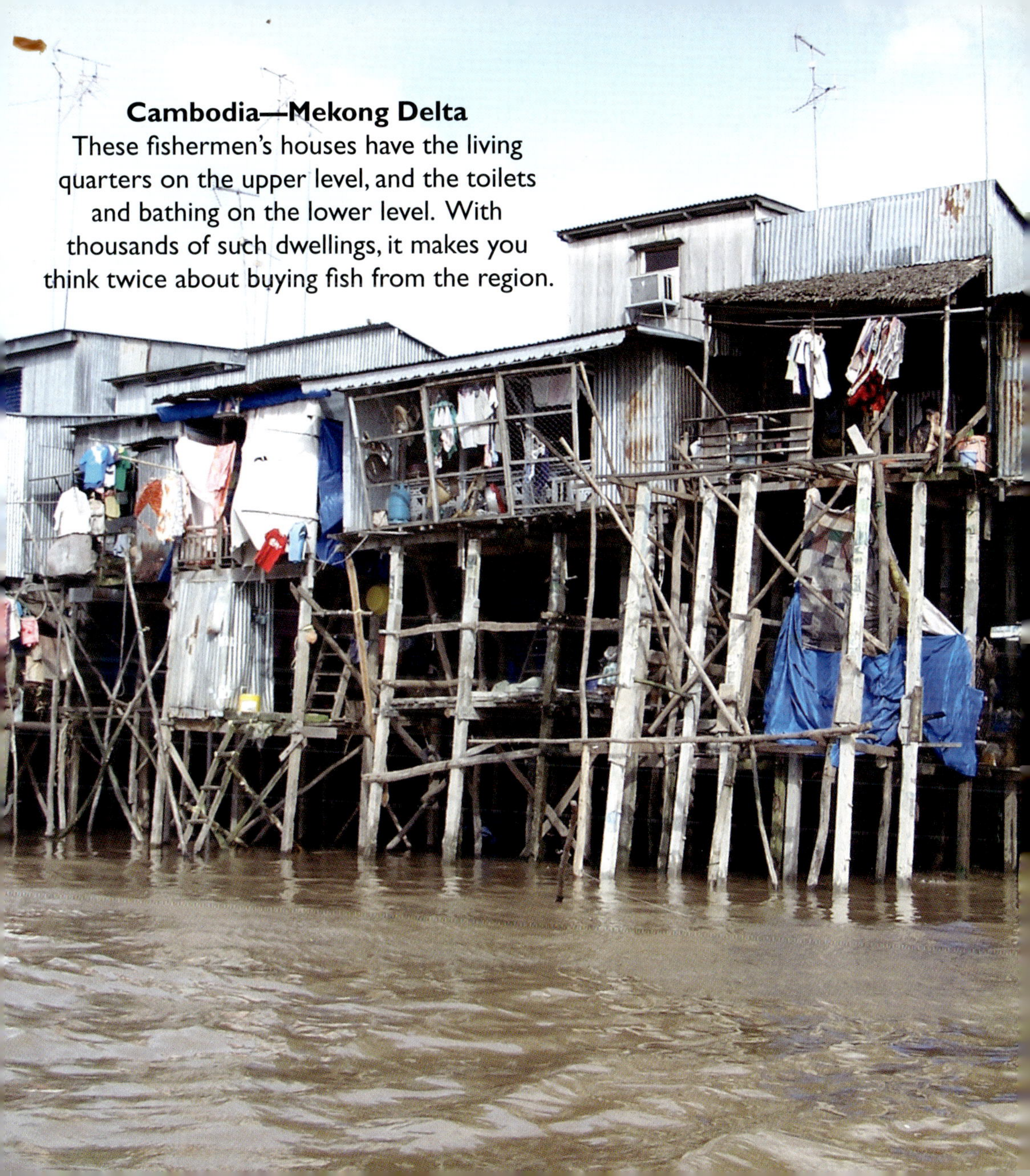

Cambodia—Mekong Delta
These fishermen's houses have the living quarters on the upper level, and the toilets and bathing on the lower level. With thousands of such dwellings, it makes you think twice about buying fish from the region.

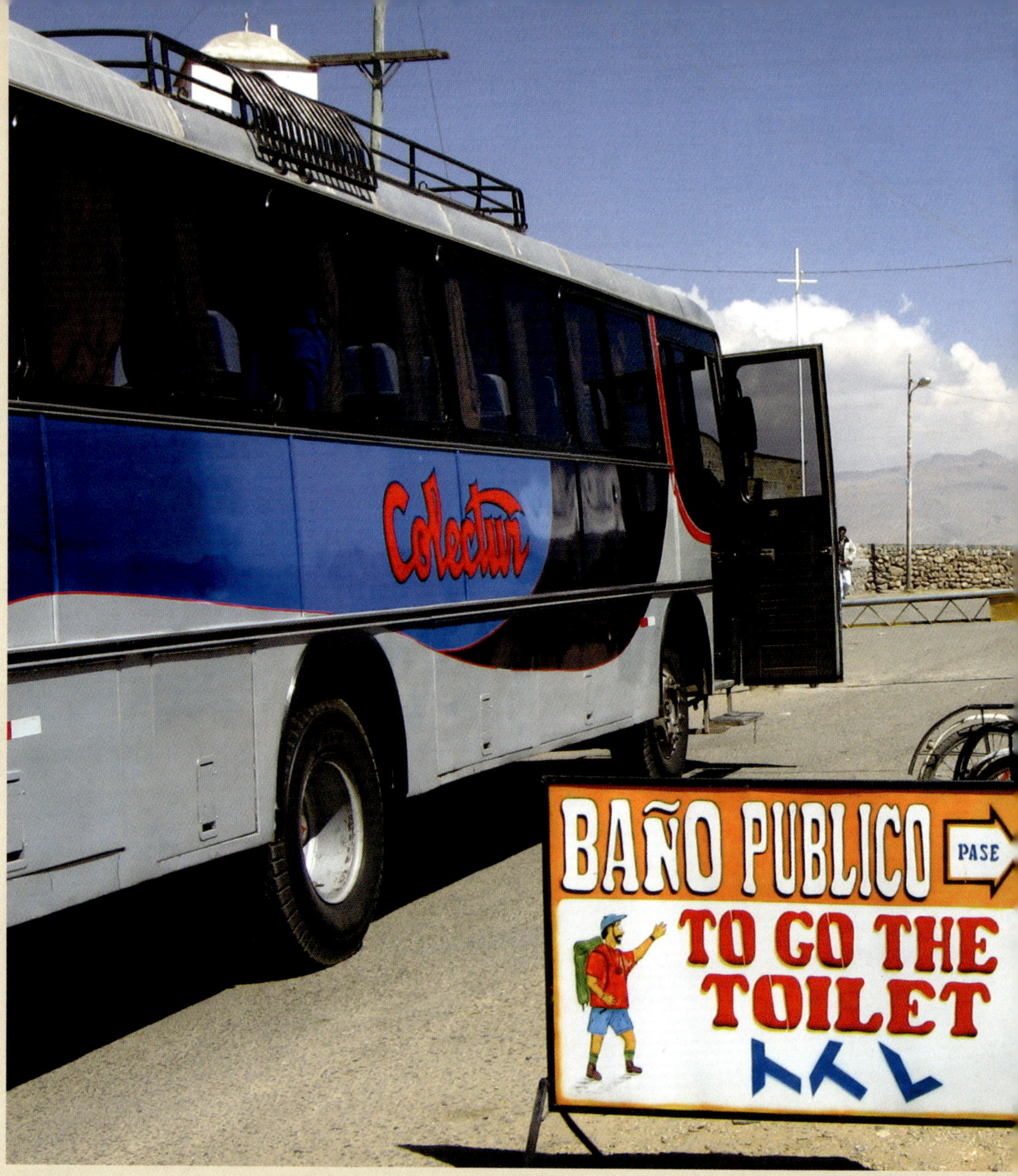
Colectur
BAÑO PUBLICO
PASE
TO GO THE TOILET

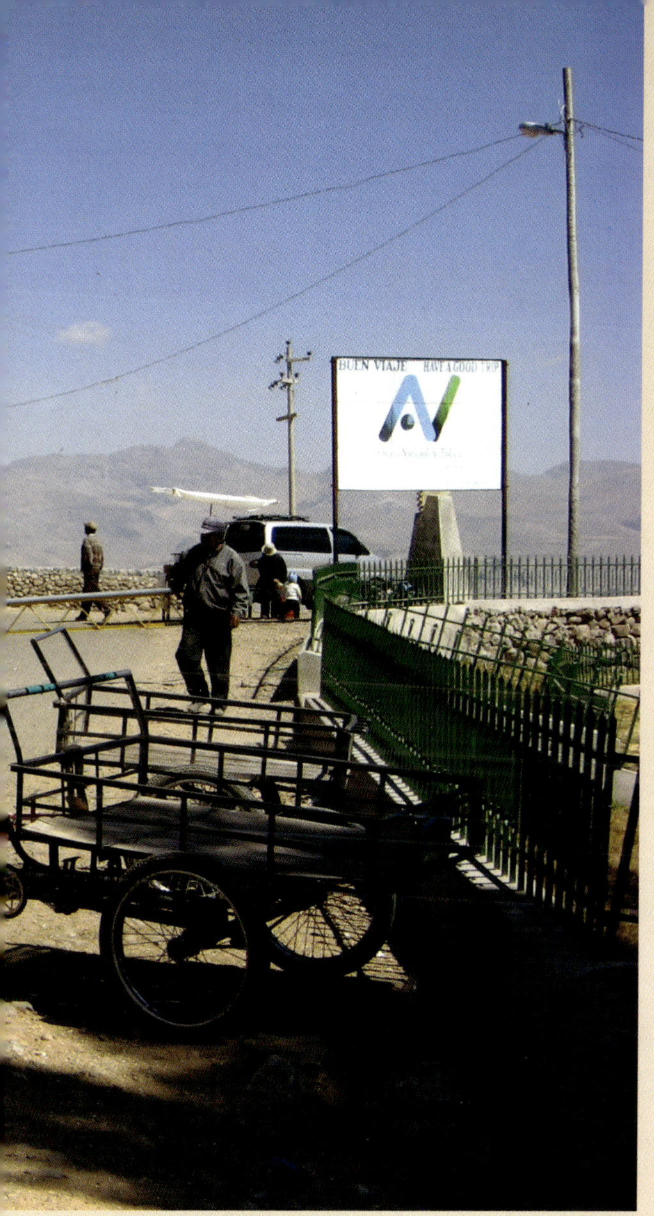

Chile—Puerto

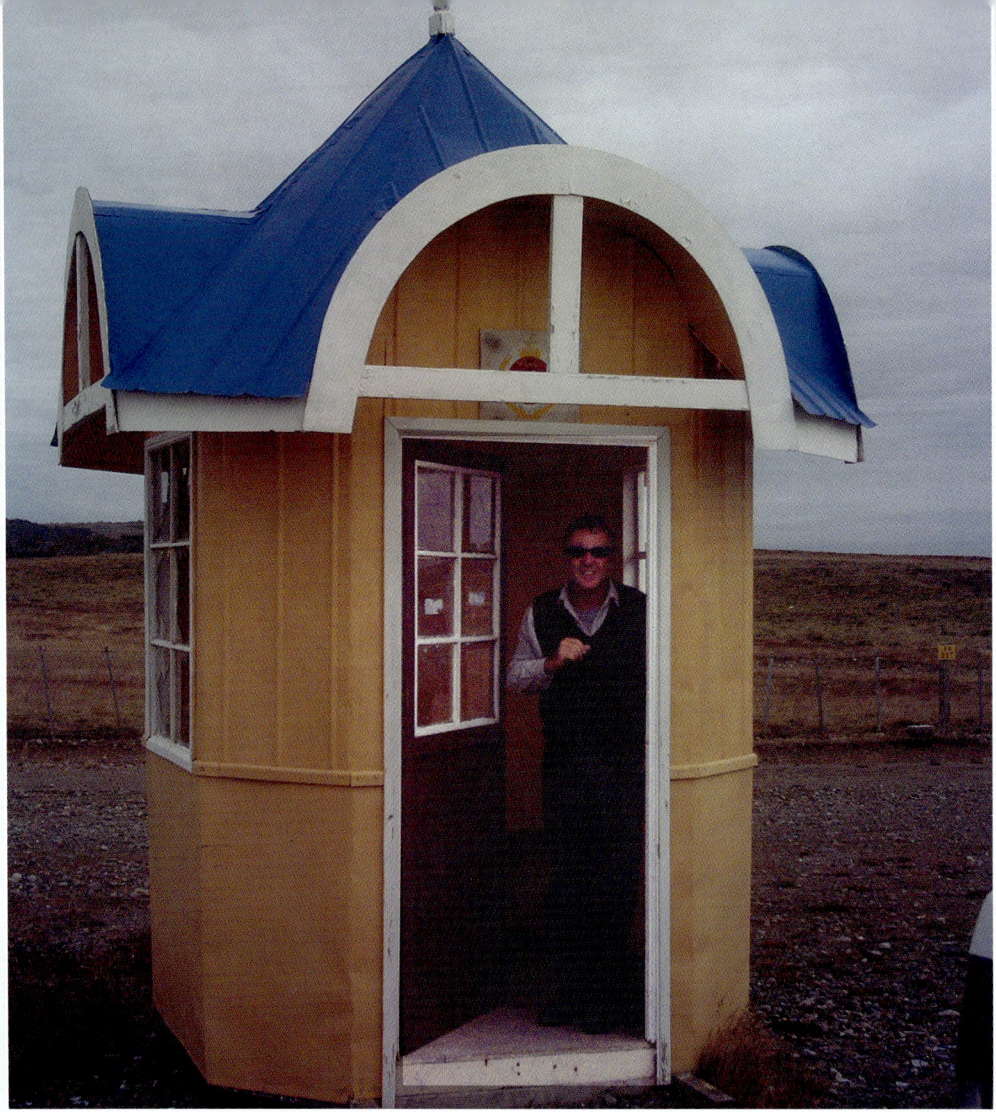

Chile—Puerto Natales

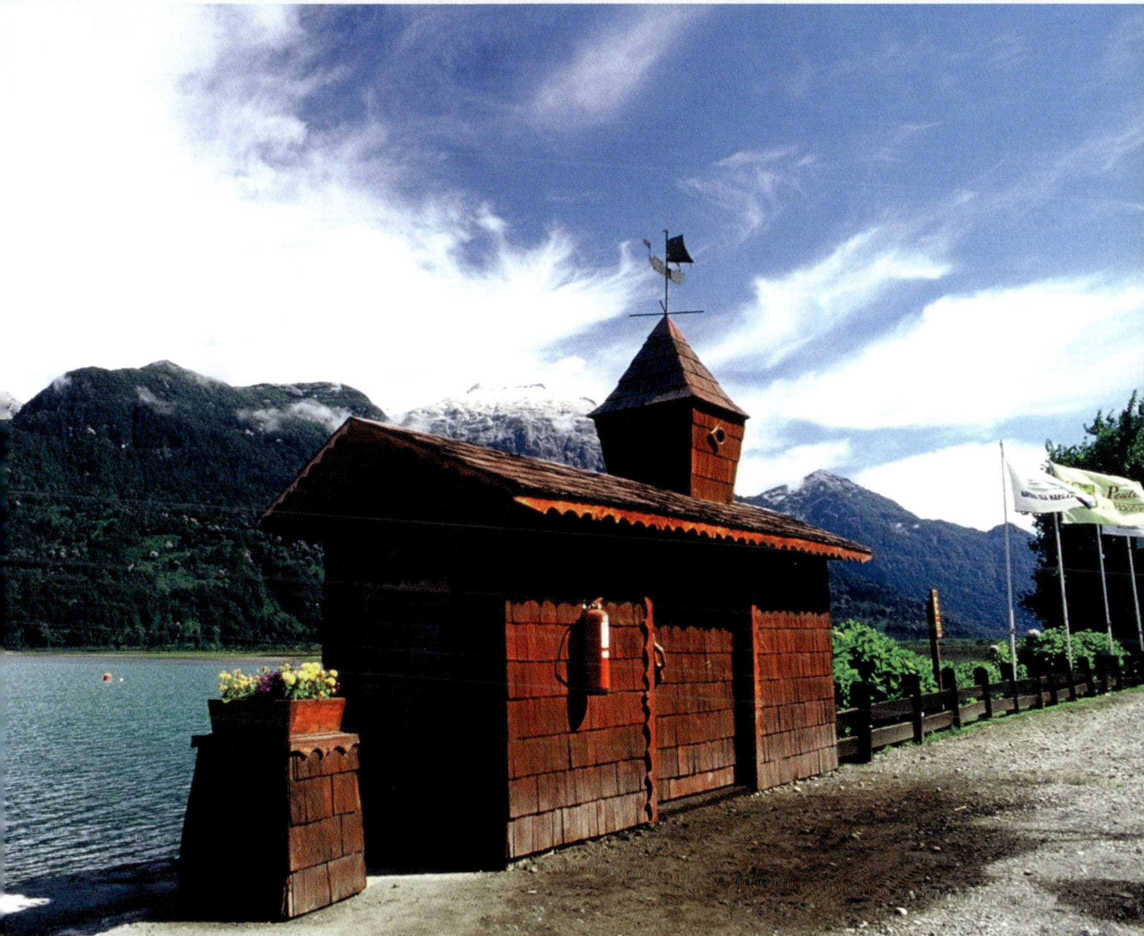

Chile—Patagonia

Beside the lakes of Patagonia sits this quaint dunny.

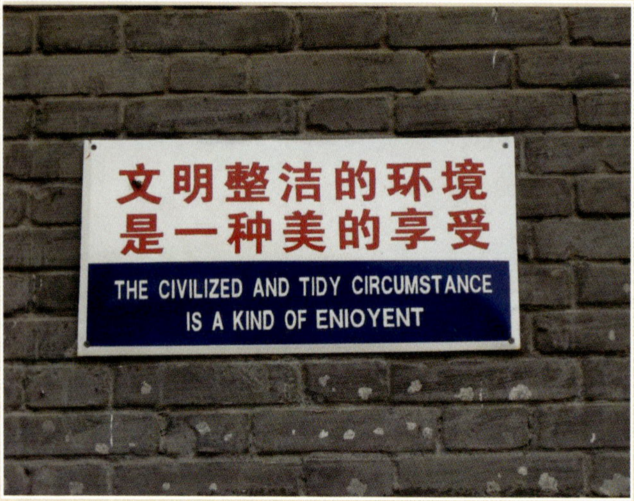
文明整洁的环境
是一种美的享受
THE CIVILIZED AND TIDY CIRCUMSTANCE
IS A KIND OF ENIOYENT

China—Xi'ian

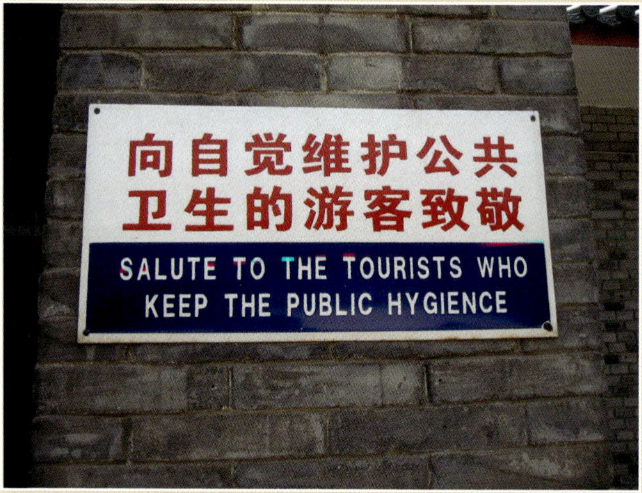
向自觉维护公共
卫生的游客致敬
SALUTE TO THE TOURISTS WHO
KEEP THE PUBLIC HYGIENCE

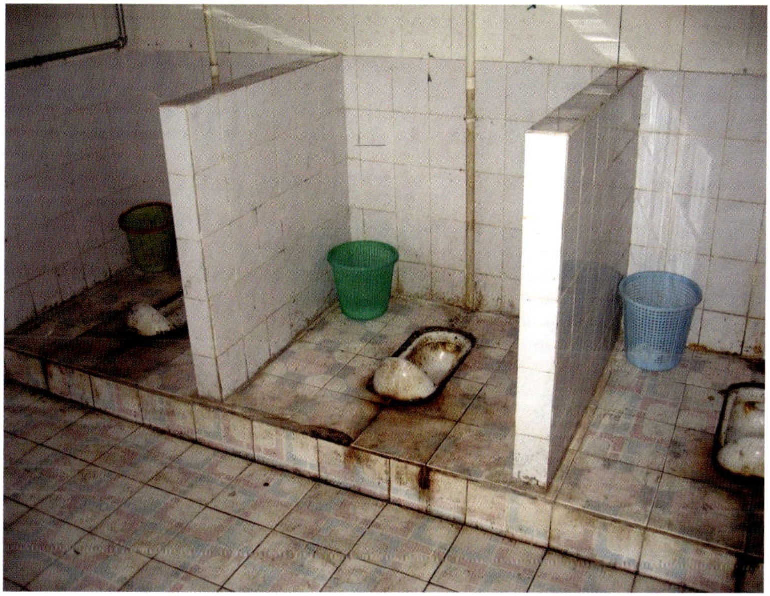

China—Xi'ian

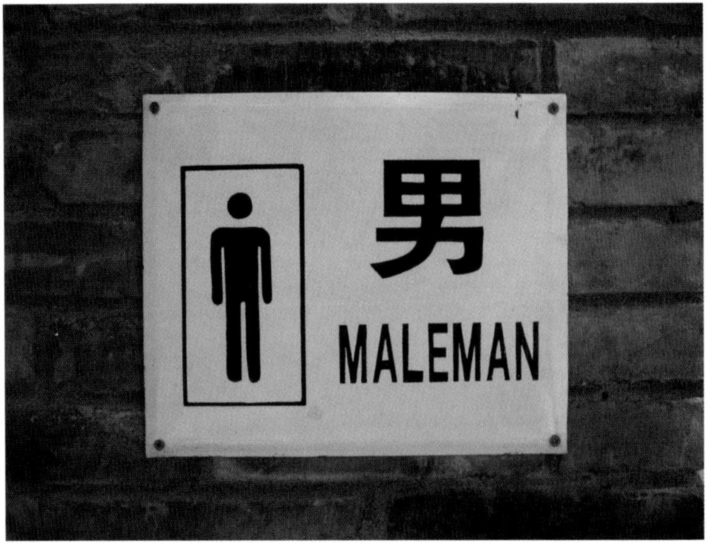

China—Xi'ian

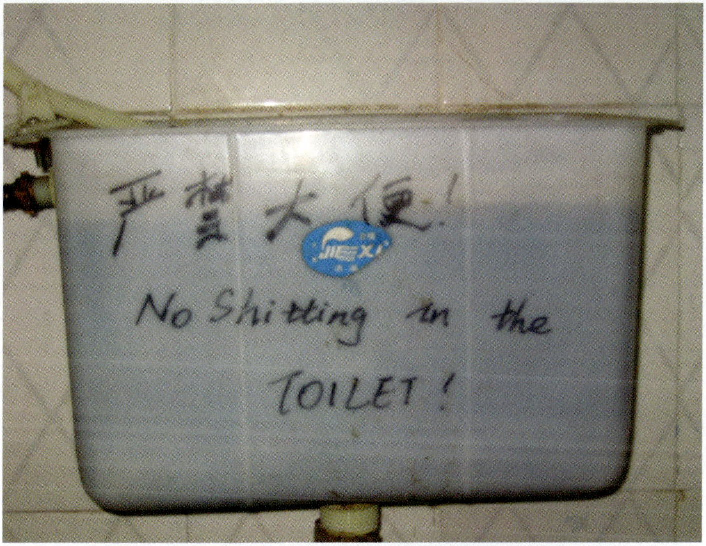

China—Dali Yunnan
What this presumably means is this:
we have a very small septic tank in this restaurant, so please do your big business at your hotel.

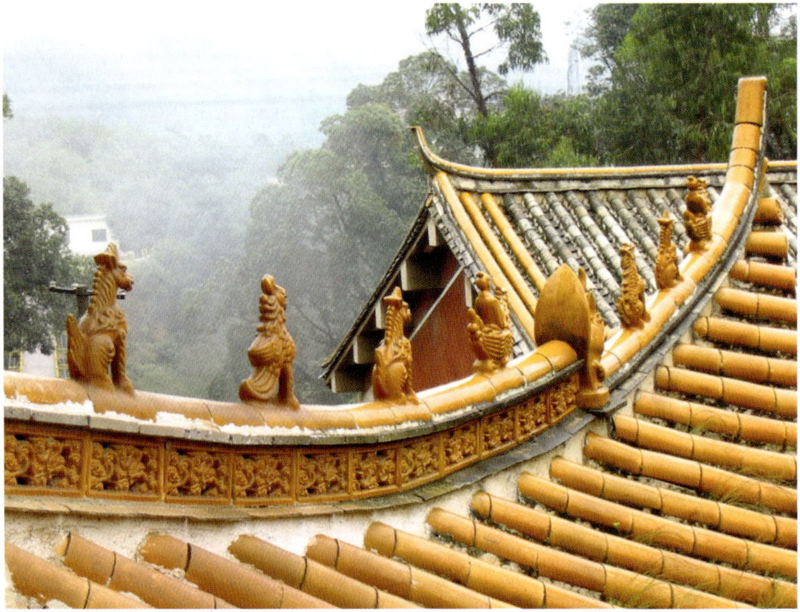

China
Toilet rooftop of Qiongzhu Si Temple near Kunning Yunnan.

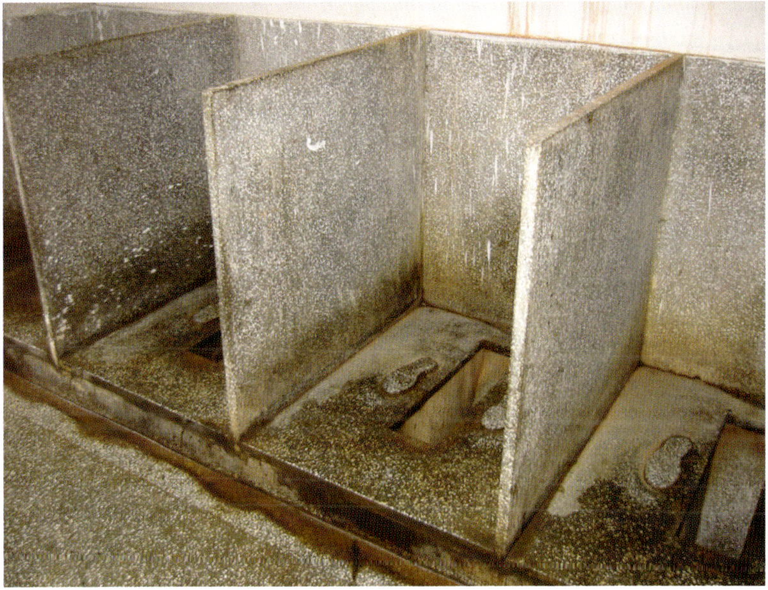

China

Inside Qiongzhu Si Temple near Kunning Yunnan.

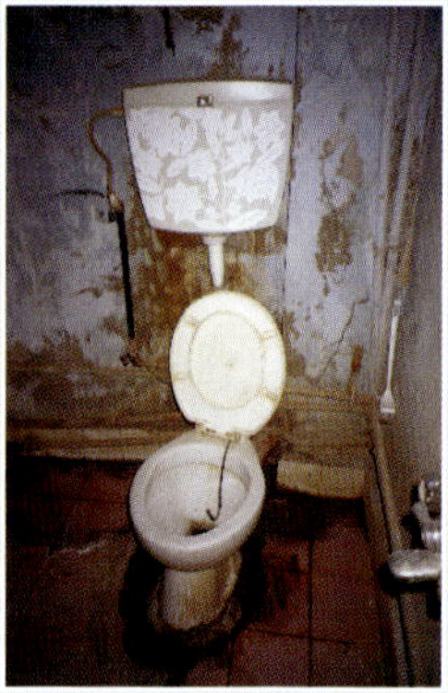

Egypt
A cheap hotel.

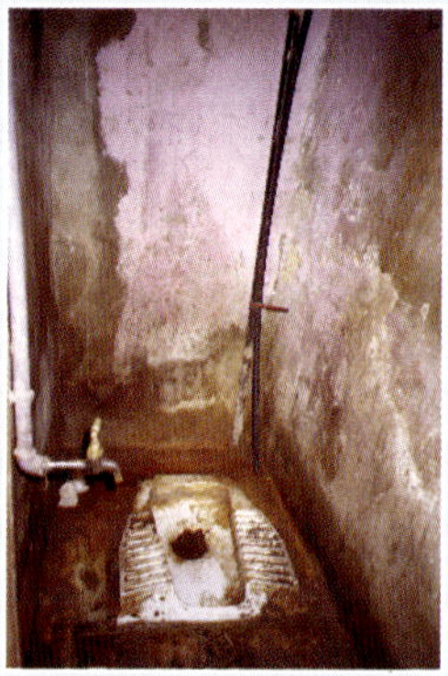

Another cheap hotel.

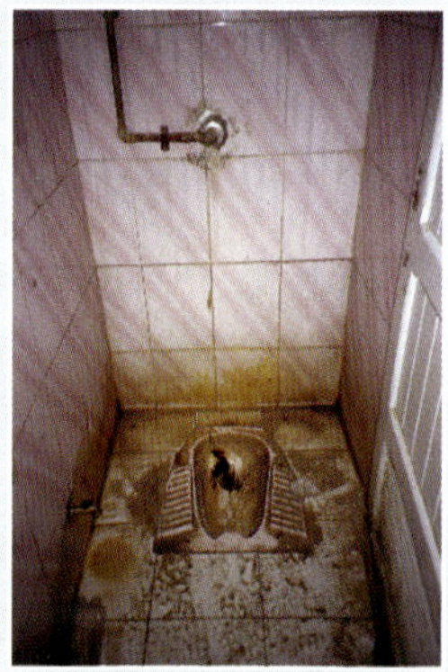

Another of those cheap hotels.

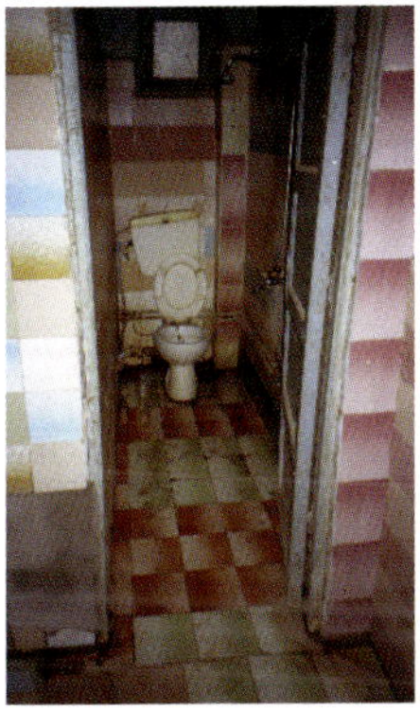

Egypt
An oasis toilet.

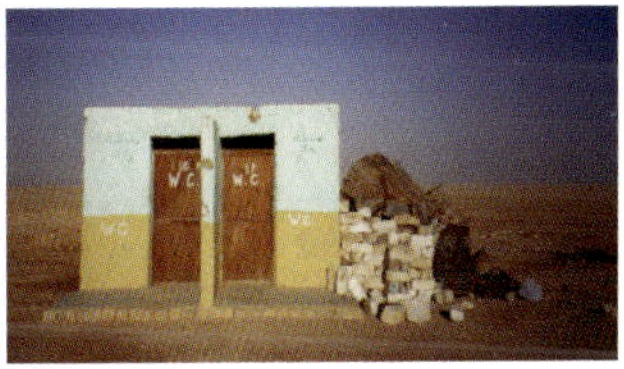

In the middle of nowhere.

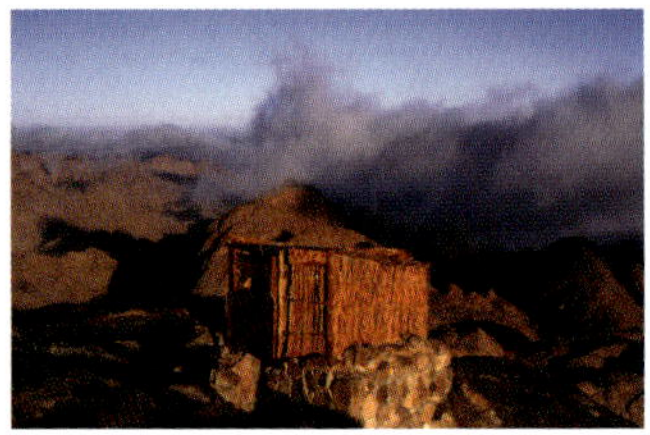

Egypt—Mt Sinai
Every dunny has a stunning view.

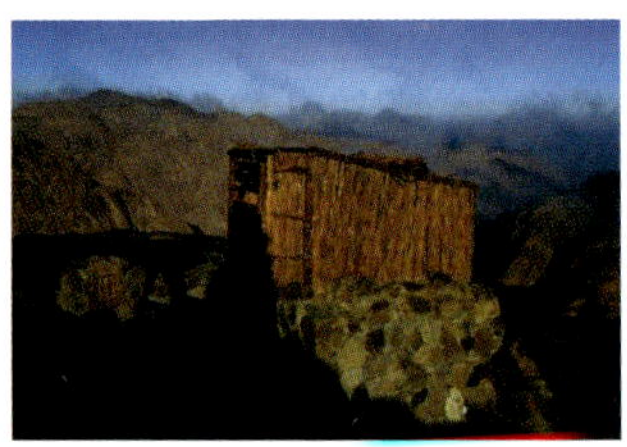

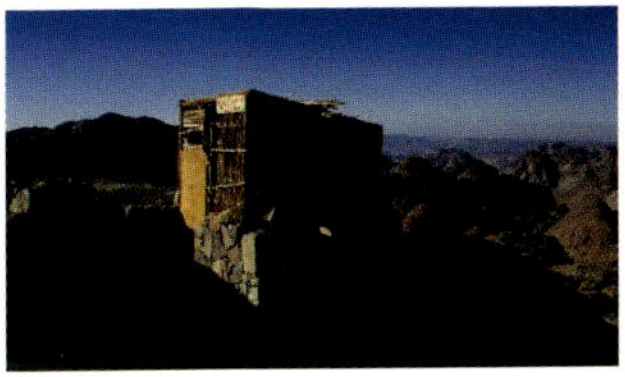

Egypt—Mt Sinai

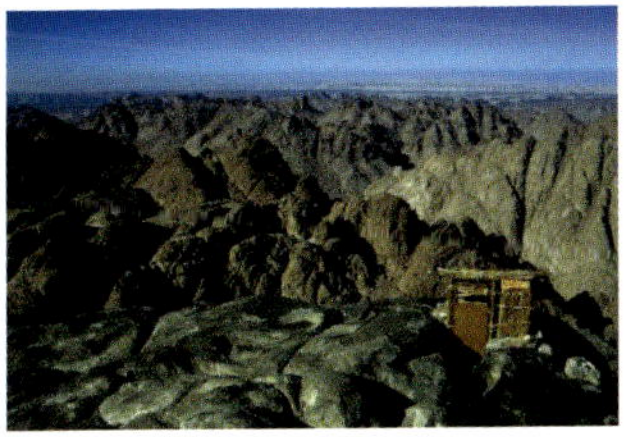

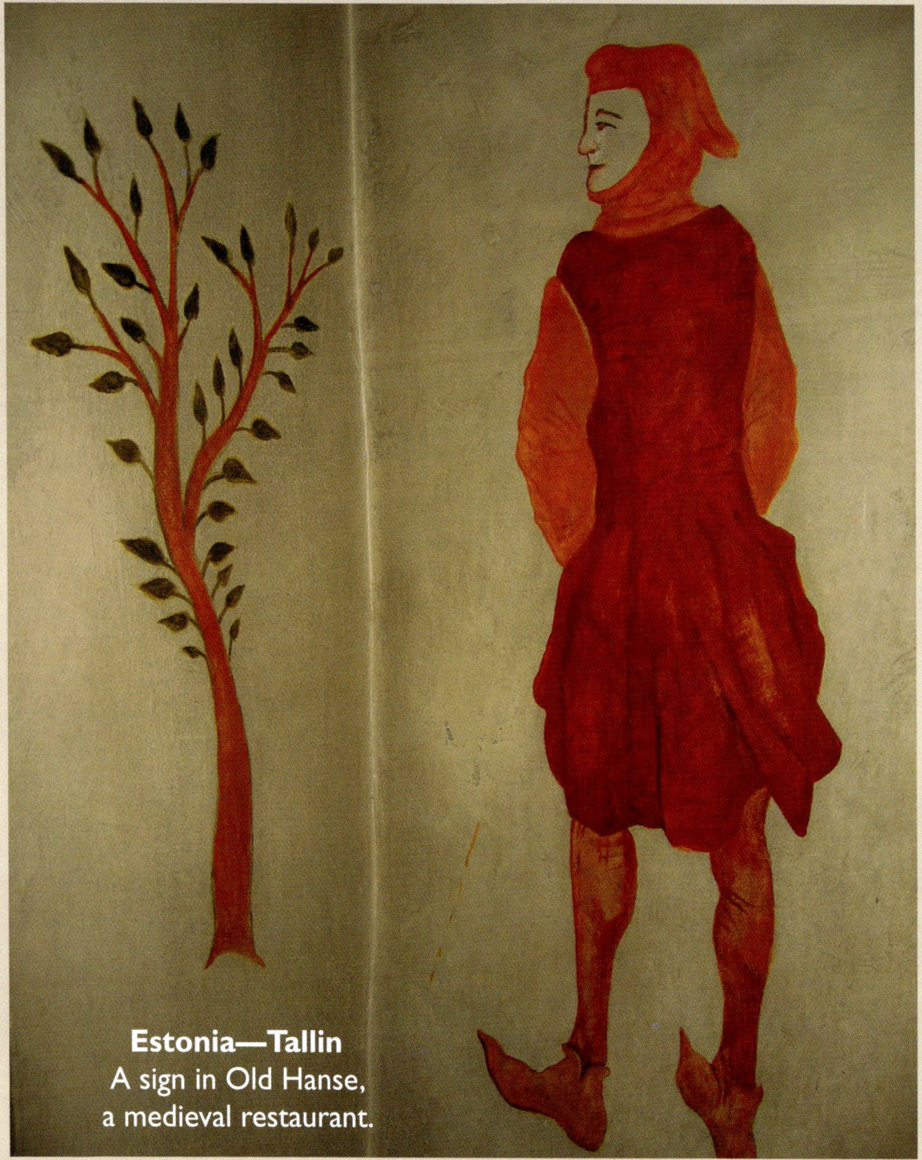

Estonia—Tallin
A sign in Old Hanse, a medieval restaurant.

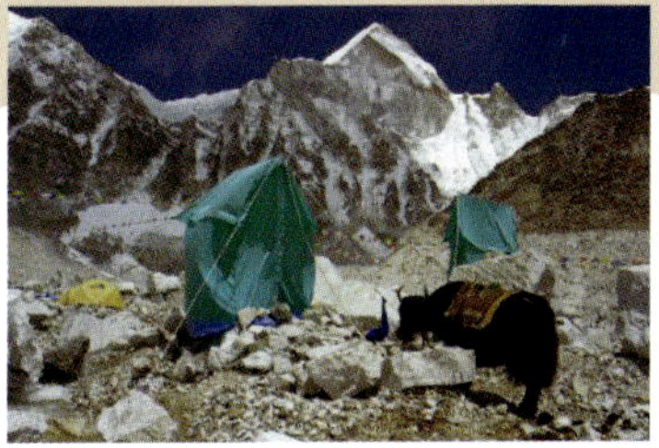

Everest

Base camp toilet with yak. This loo is at the base camp in a small tent. A simple blue container is what one's business drops into. Then a friendly and highly efficient Sherpa takes it away—they can't let it pollute the local water from the glacier. At the time of taking this photo there were 36 groups waiting to go up Everest, and as the wind was too strong for a safe departure, over 200 kilometres per hour on top of Everest, they all had to wait … and that's a lot of human excrement that has to be carried away.

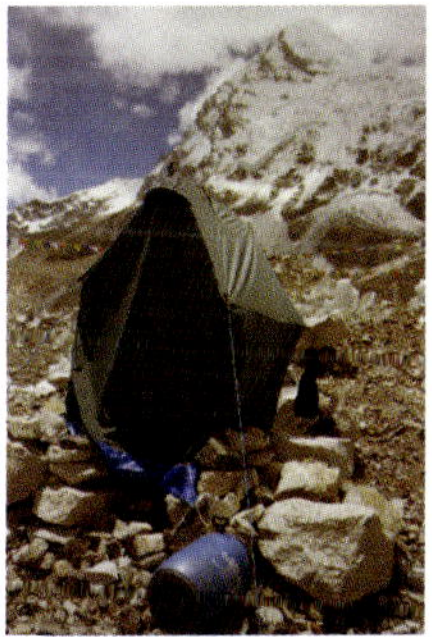

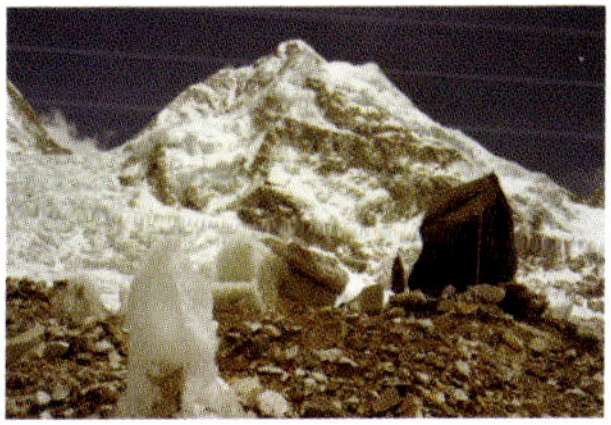

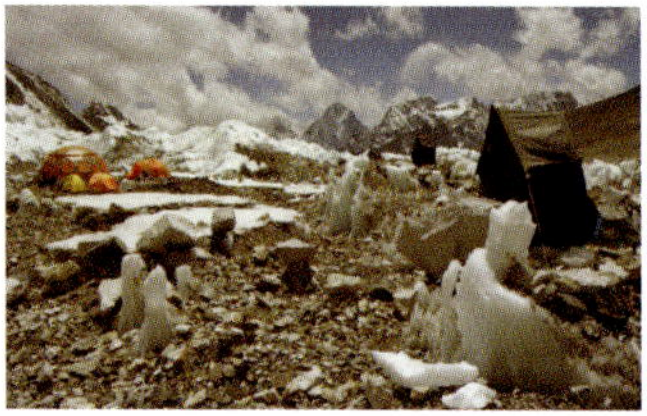

Everest
Base camp.

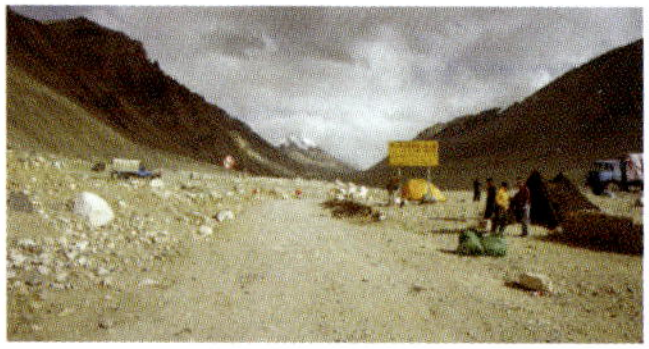

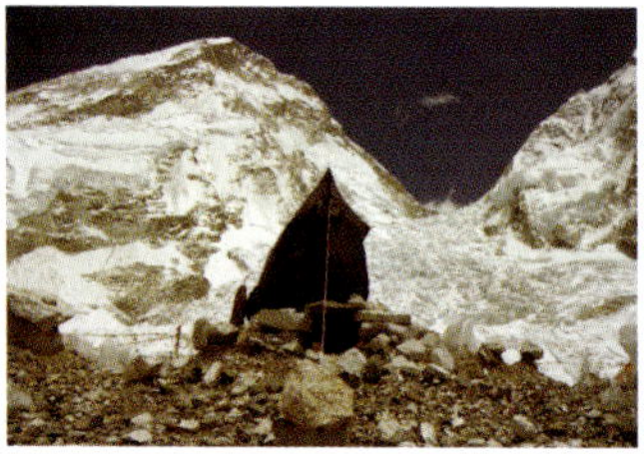

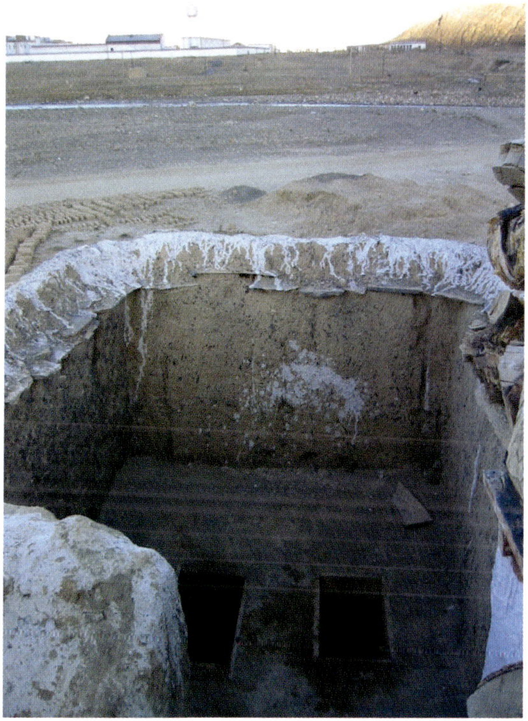

Everest
En route to base camp.

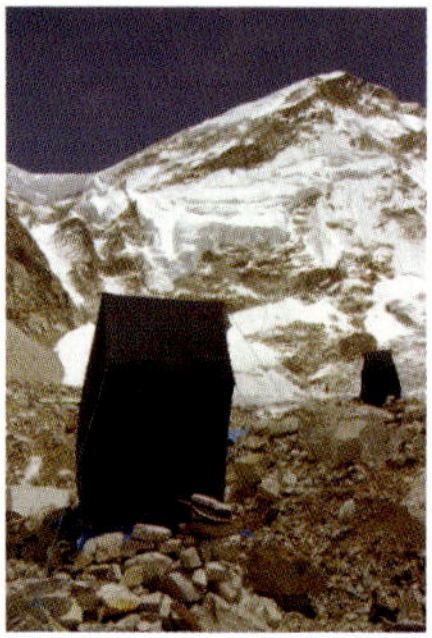

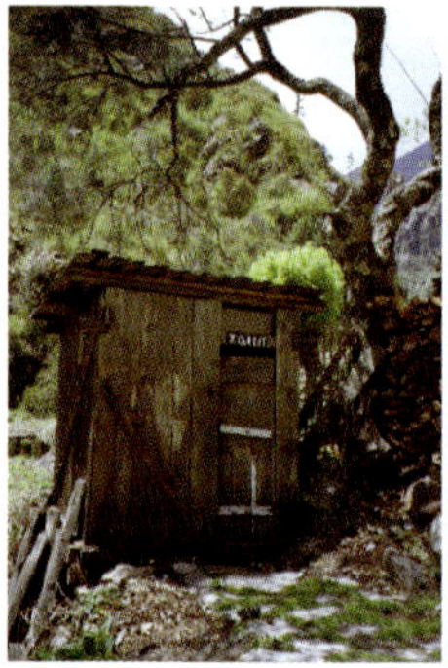

Everest Base camp toilets.

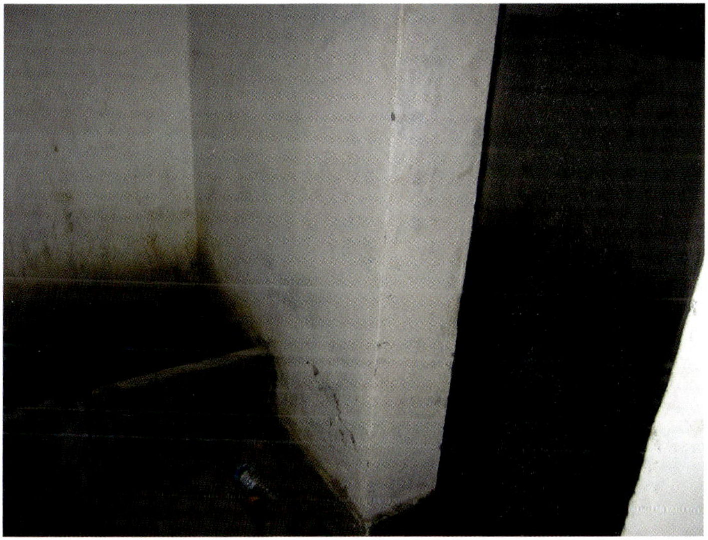

Everest
Base camp Tibet side, 5200 metres.

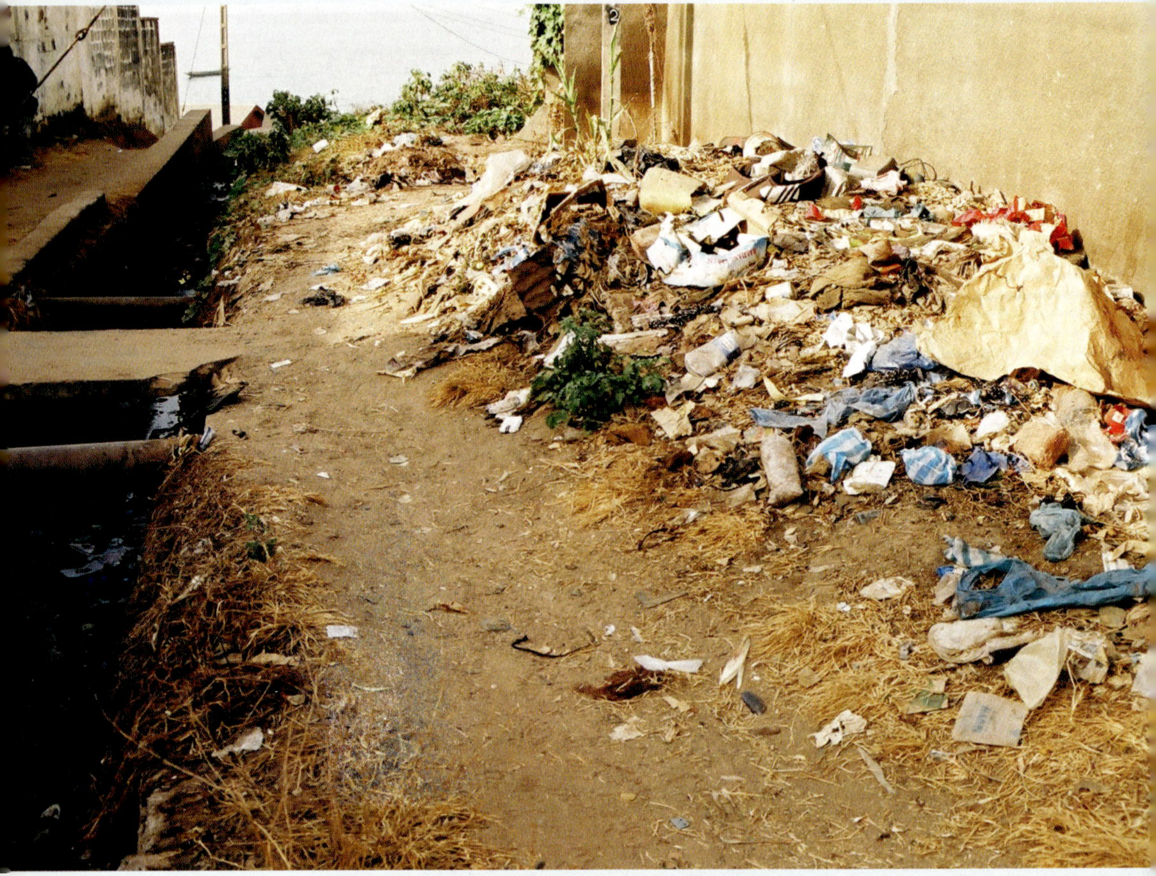

The Gambia—Bakau
An open sewer leads to the ocean. It's also an opportunity to discard plastic and other rubbish.

The Gambia—Brikama

It's a regular occurrence throughout much of Africa to see people relieve themselves on or near any wall. This one, nearby the main bus station was no exception. 'No Urine' means what it says. 'No Dumping' doesn't!

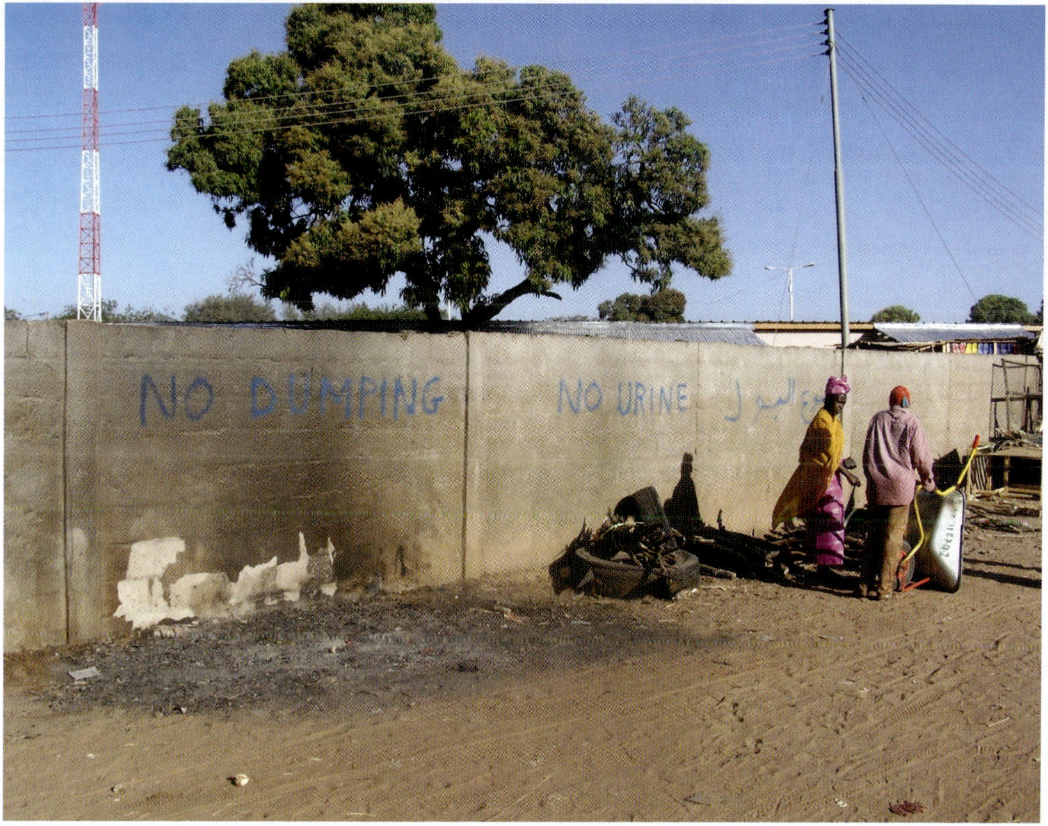

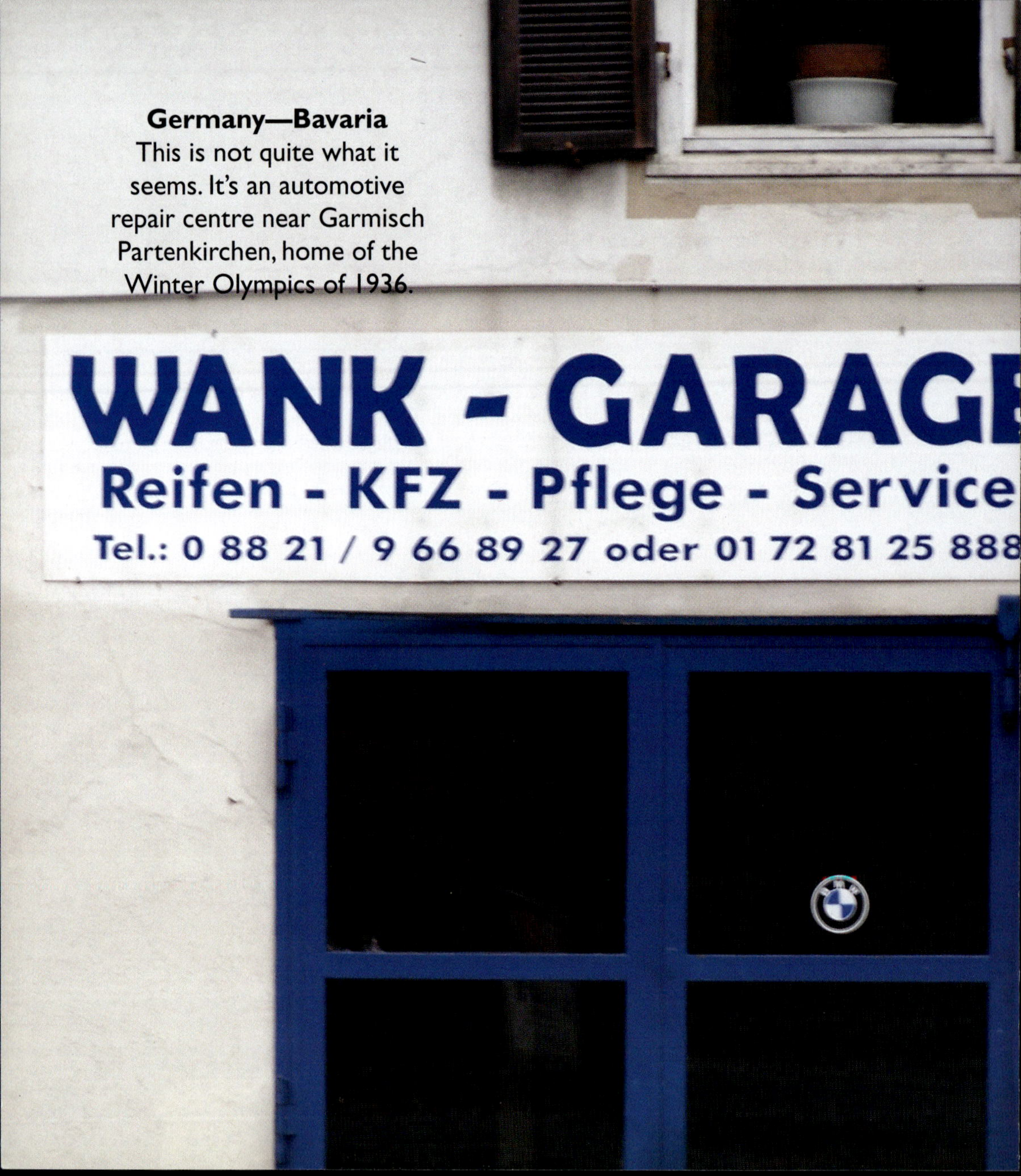

Germany—Bavaria
This is not quite what it seems. It's an automotive repair centre near Garmisch Partenkirchen, home of the Winter Olympics of 1936.

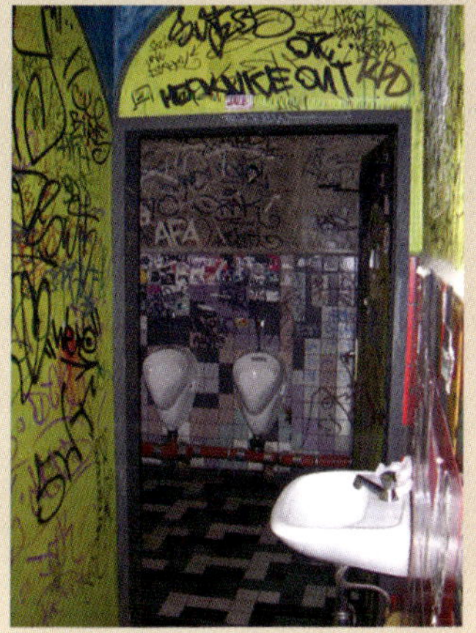

Germany—Berlin
Gents' dunny.

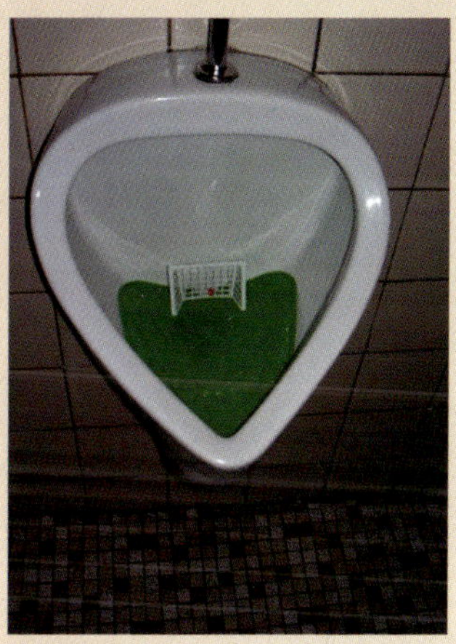

Germany—Detmold
Pub called *Der Krug*.

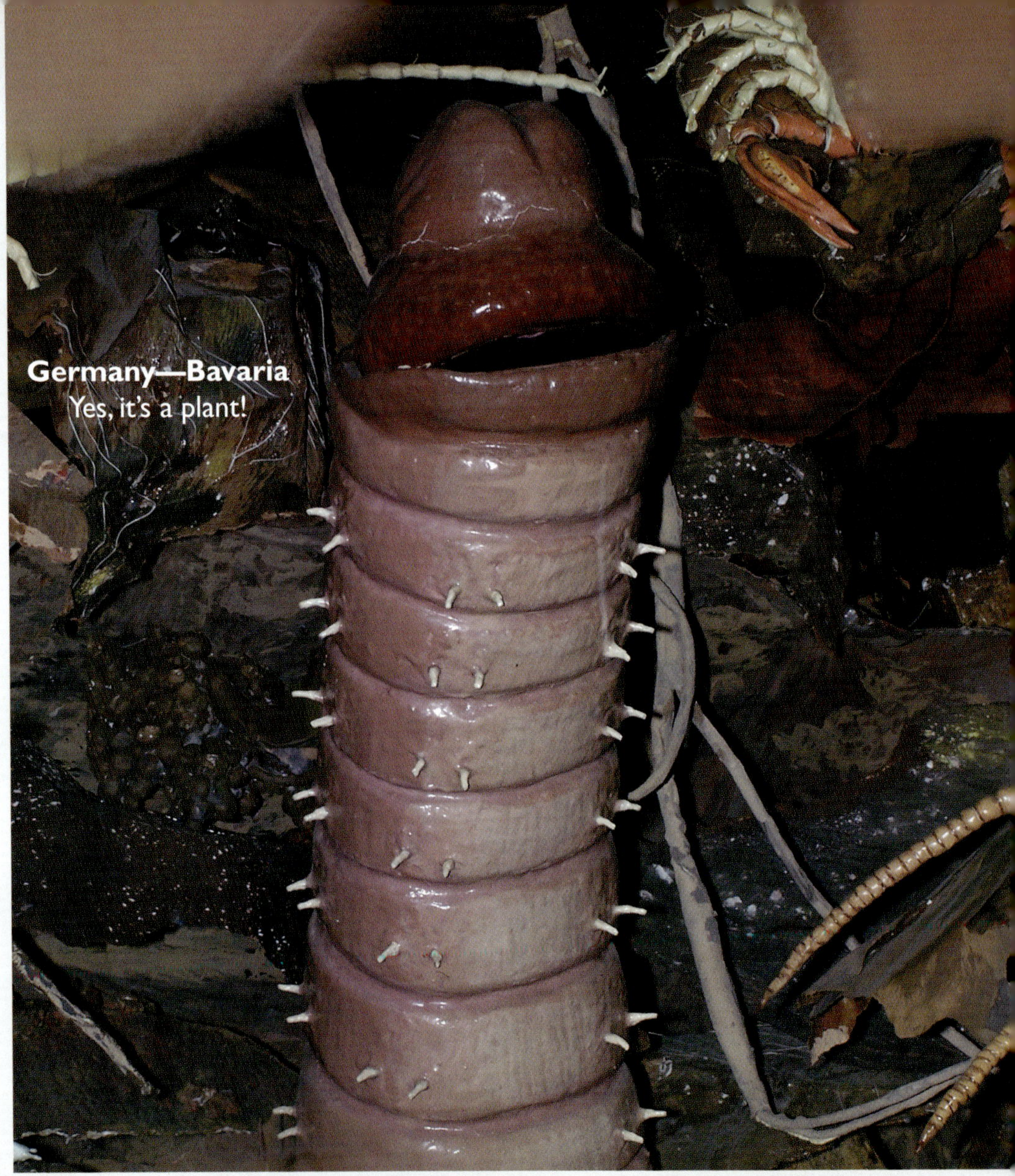

Germany—Bavaria
Yes, it's a plant!

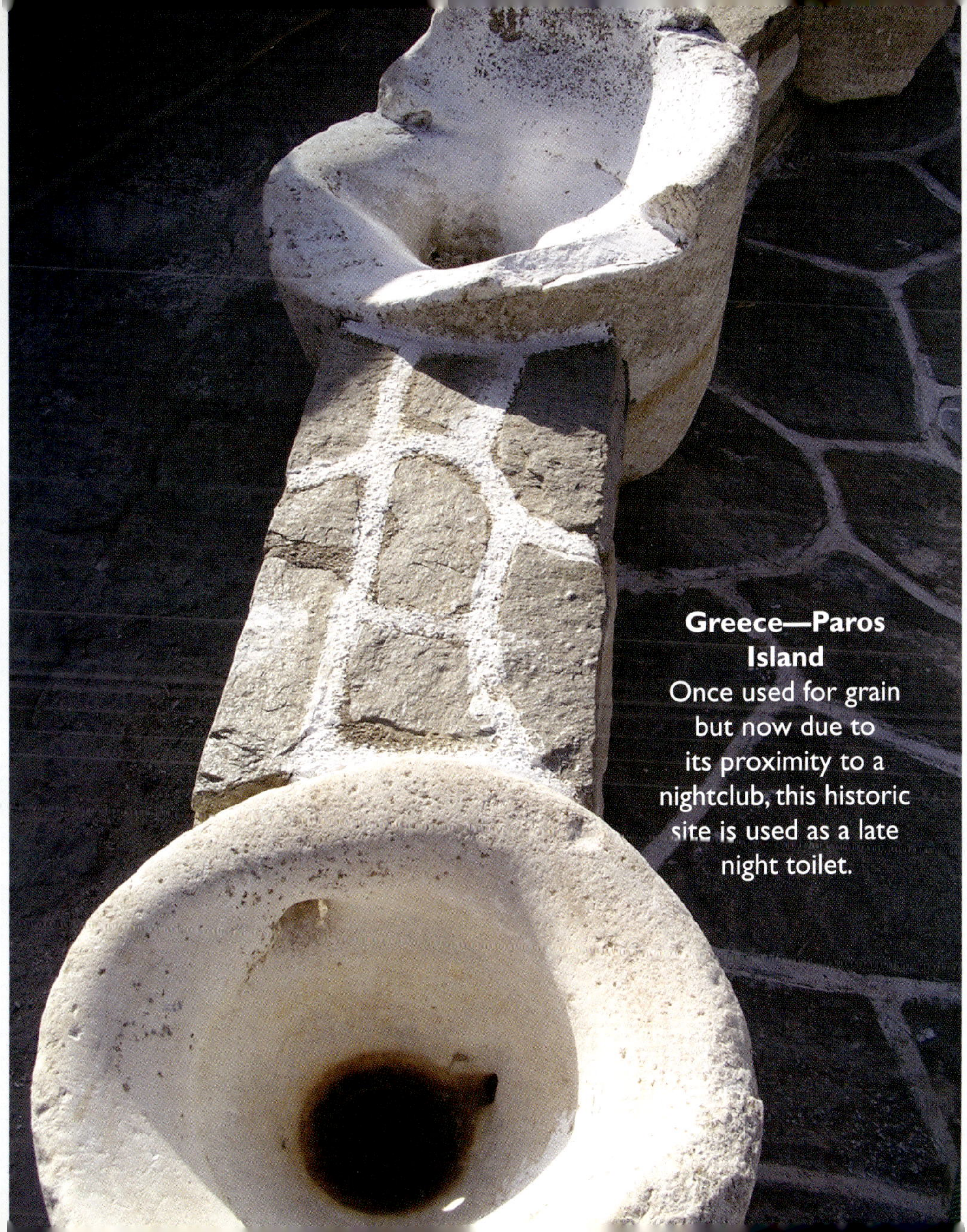

Greece—Paros Island

Once used for grain but now due to its proximity to a nightclub, this historic site is used as a late night toilet.

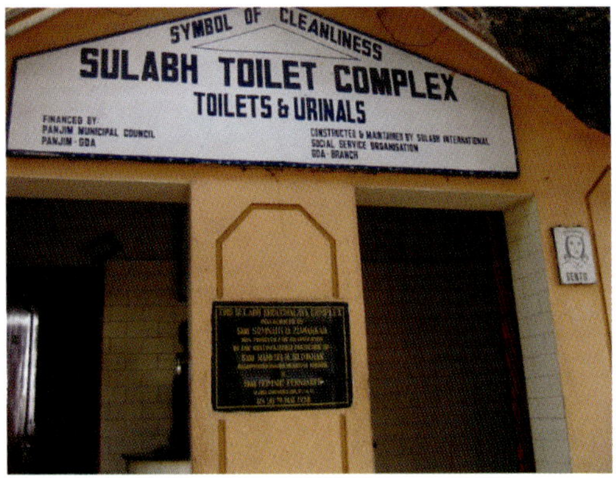
SYMBOL OF CLEANLINESS
SULABH TOILET COMPLEX
TOILETS & URINALS
FINANCED BY:
PANJIM MUNICIPAL COUNCIL
PANJIM - GOA

India—Goa

Latvia—Riga

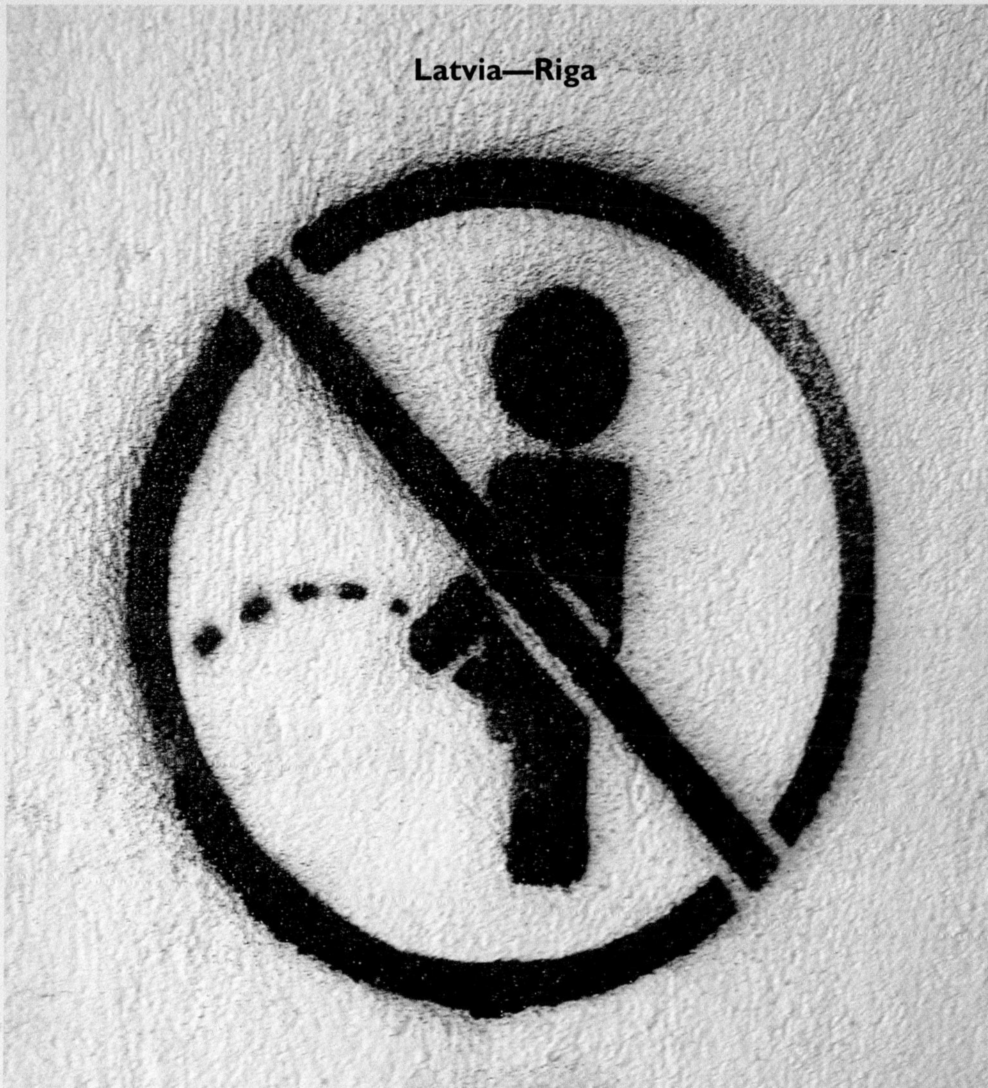

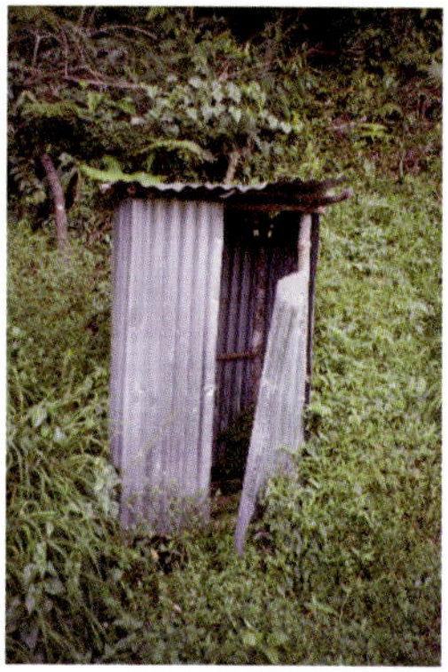

Malaysia
In the jungle.

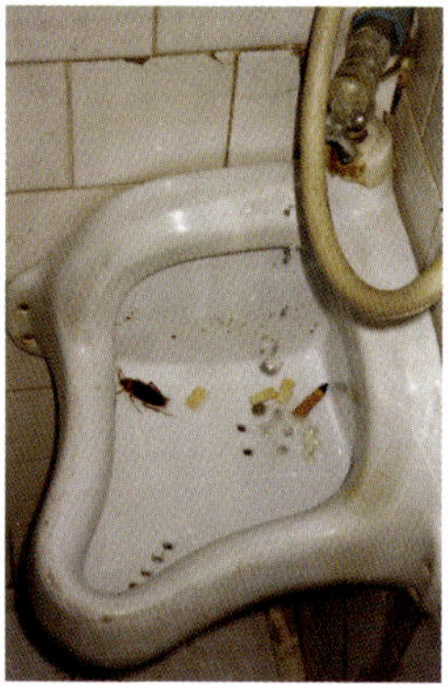

Cockroach trapped with no way out.

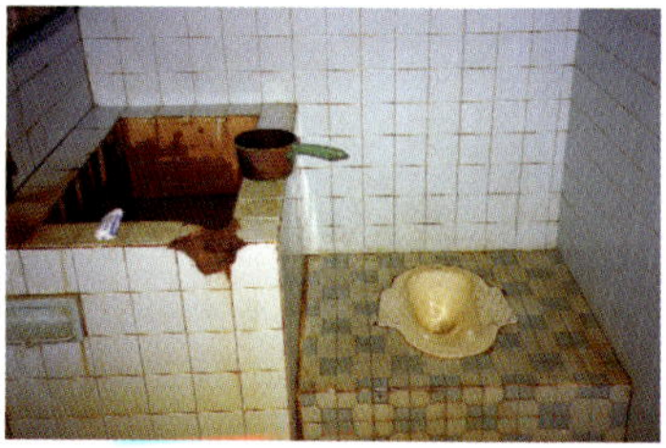

A toilet in the Melaka region.

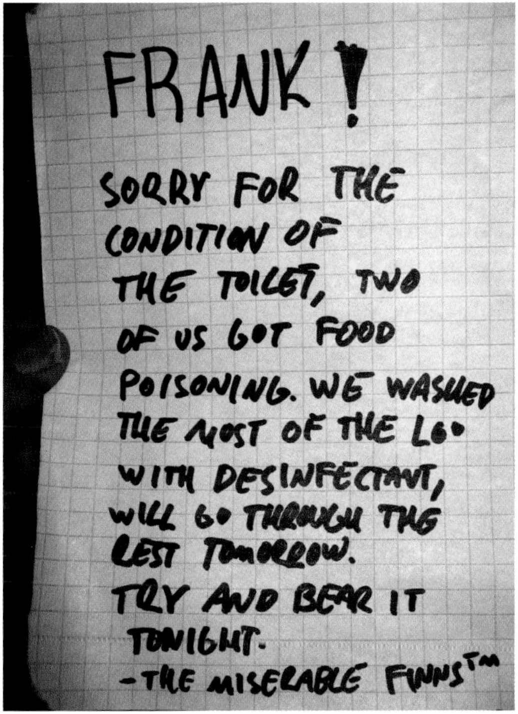

Mongolia—Ulan Bator
Traveller's note.

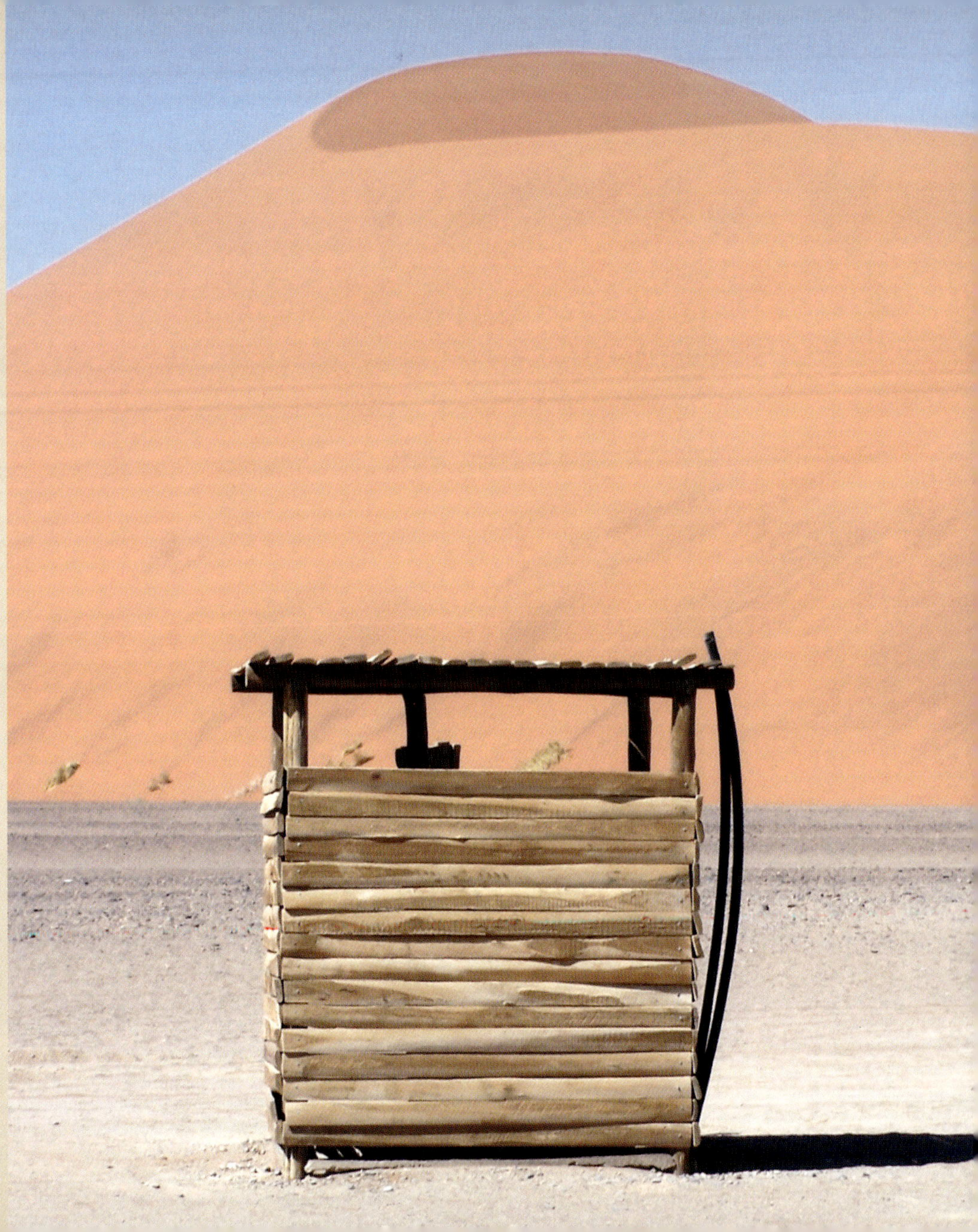

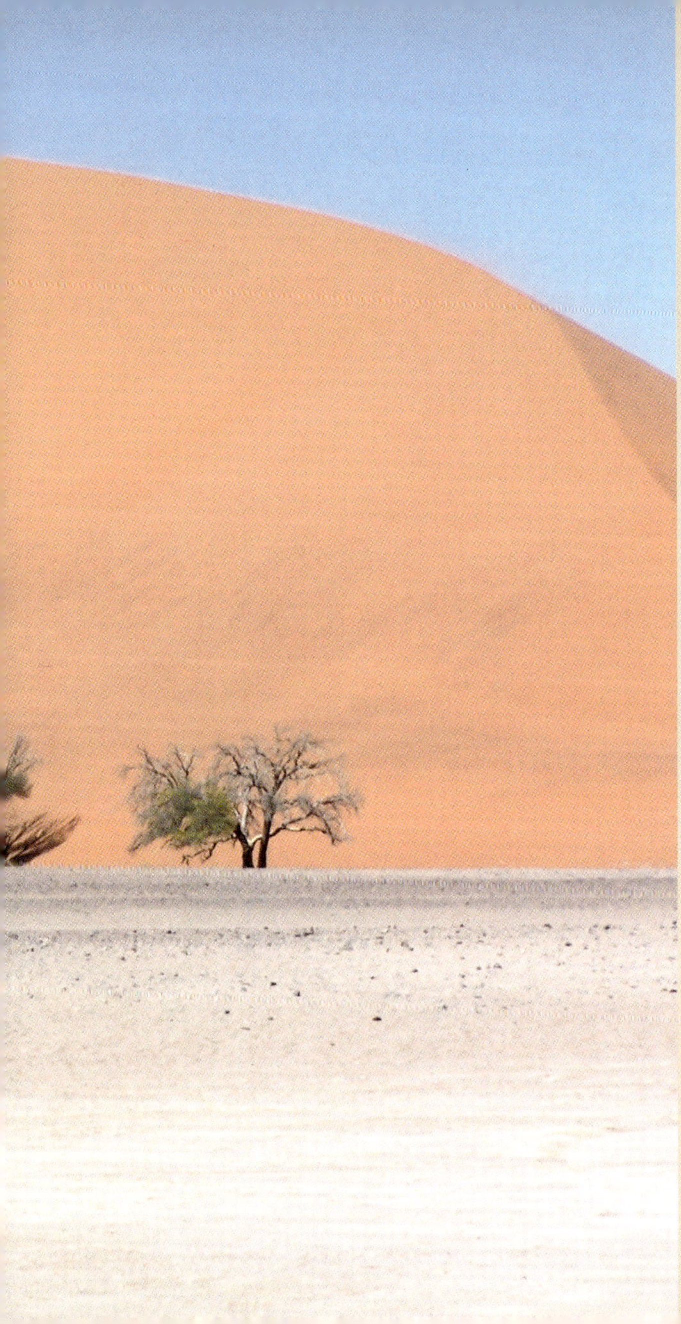

Namibia
This out-of-the-way spot was en route to the Deadvlei in Namibia, an area where ground temperatures regularly exceed 60 degrees Celsius and where the dramatic windswept sand dunes change shape daily. This toilet was not just the only dunny for a hundred kilometres, but the only building.

Nepal
A catchy name—
turn the page to see the
bath-house and toilet.

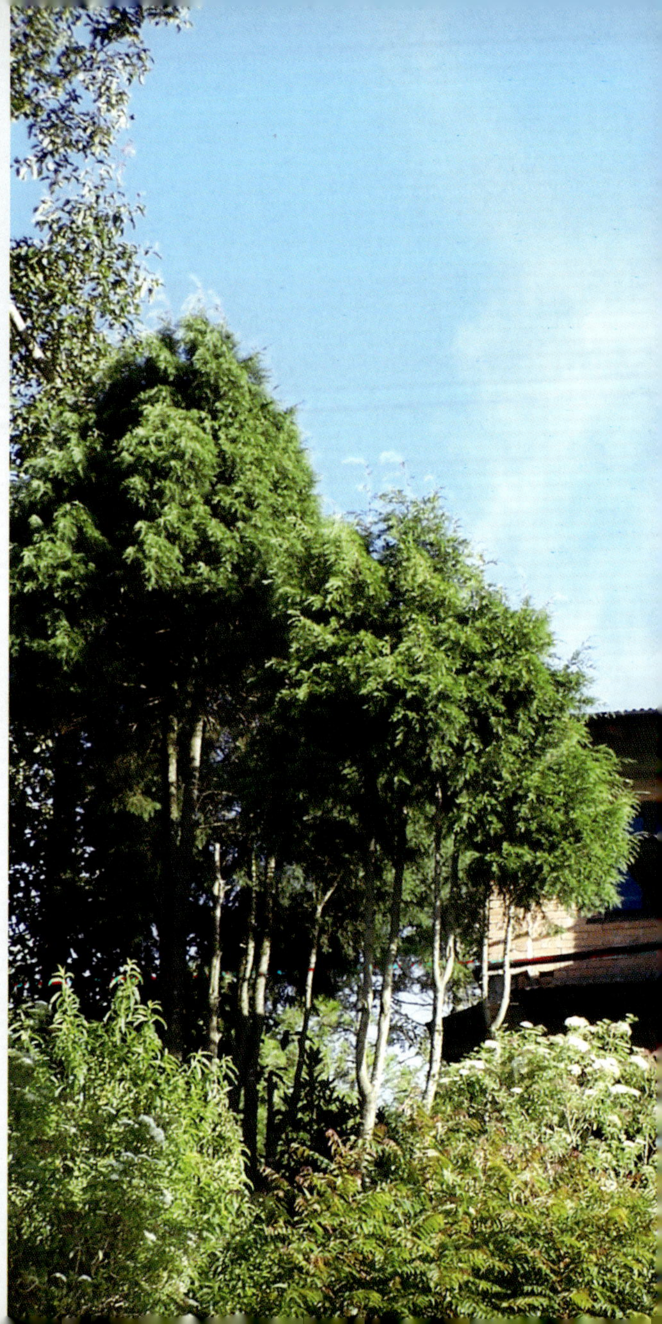

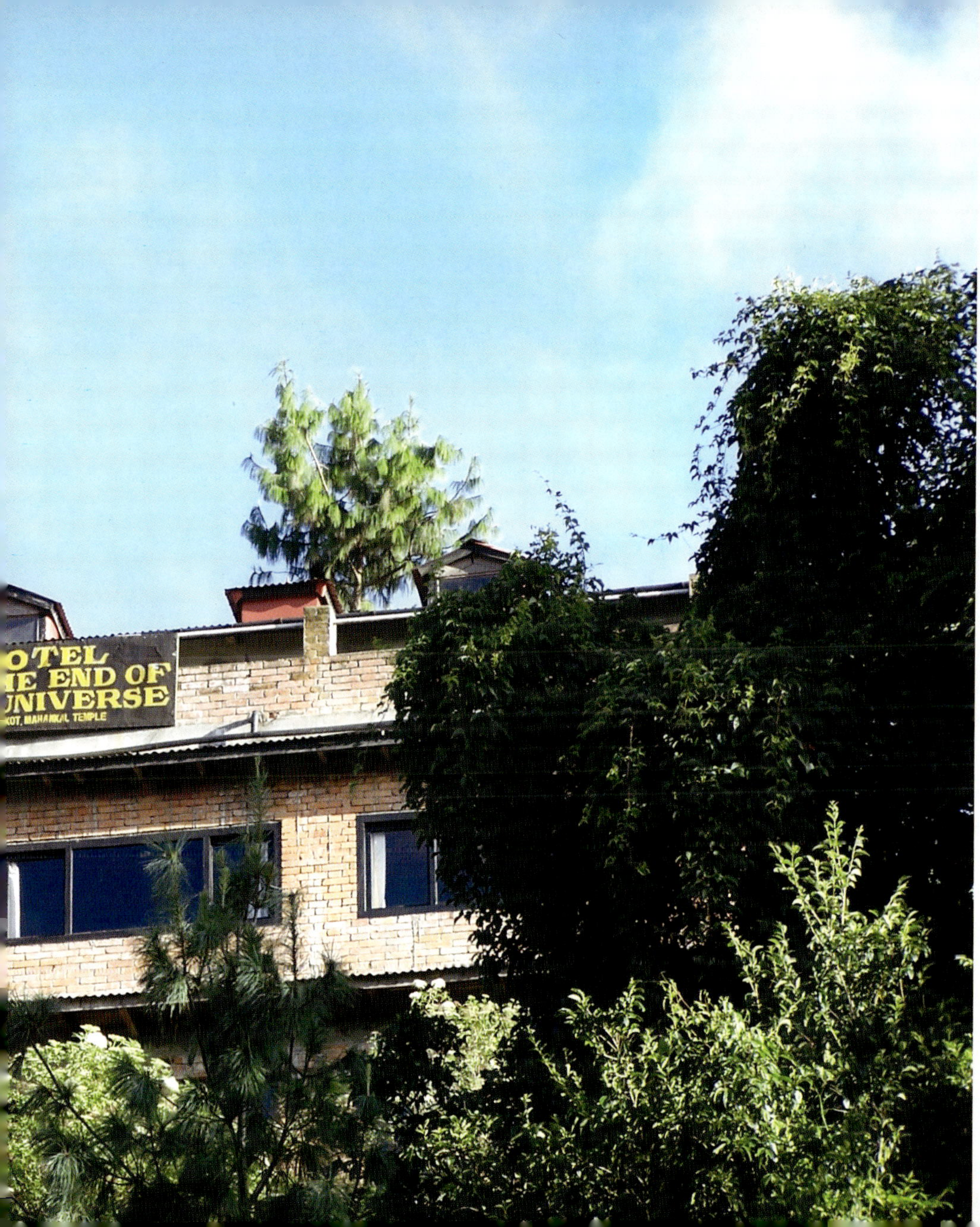
OTEL
E END OF
NIVERSE
KOT, MAHANKAL TEMPLE

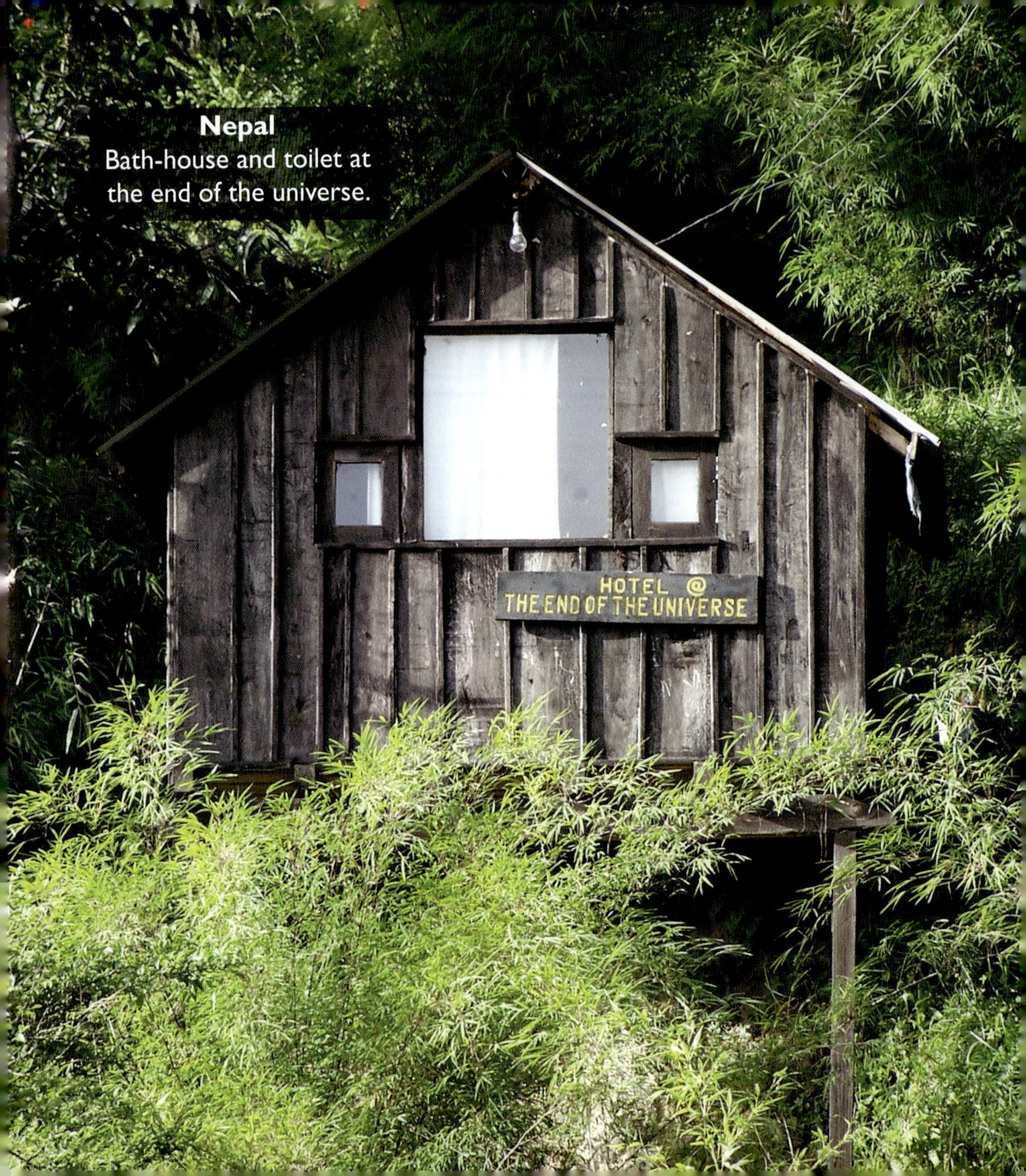

Nepal
Bath-house and toilet at the end of the universe.

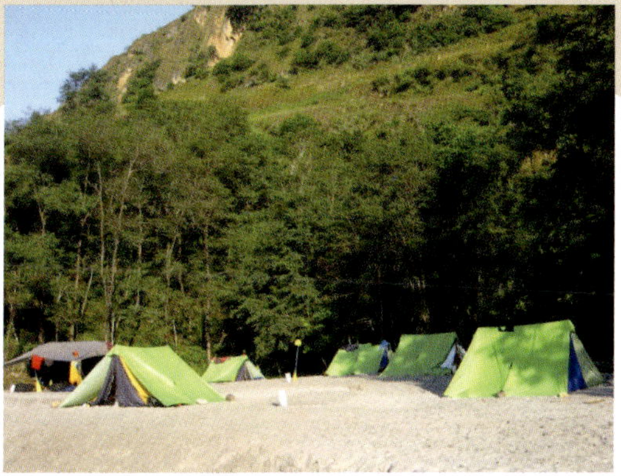

Nepal—Kali Gandaki River

This is a camping scene on a beach on the Kali Gandaki River south of Pokhara. A hole is dug in the back of the campground, and the paddle marks the spot. The helmet is the key: when the helmet is on the paddle, it's vacant, and when the helmet is gone, it's busy.

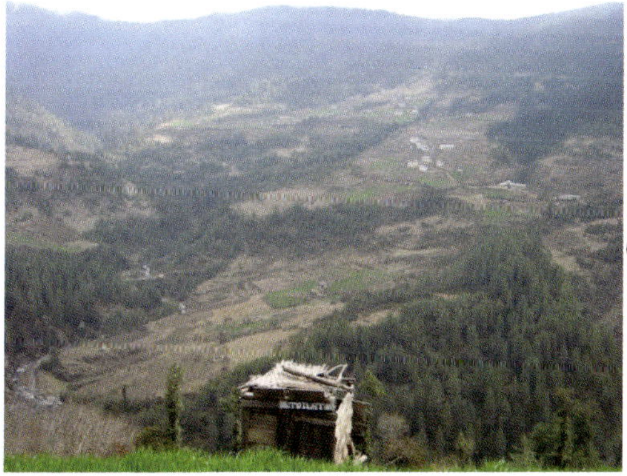

Every toilet in Nepal offers a view.

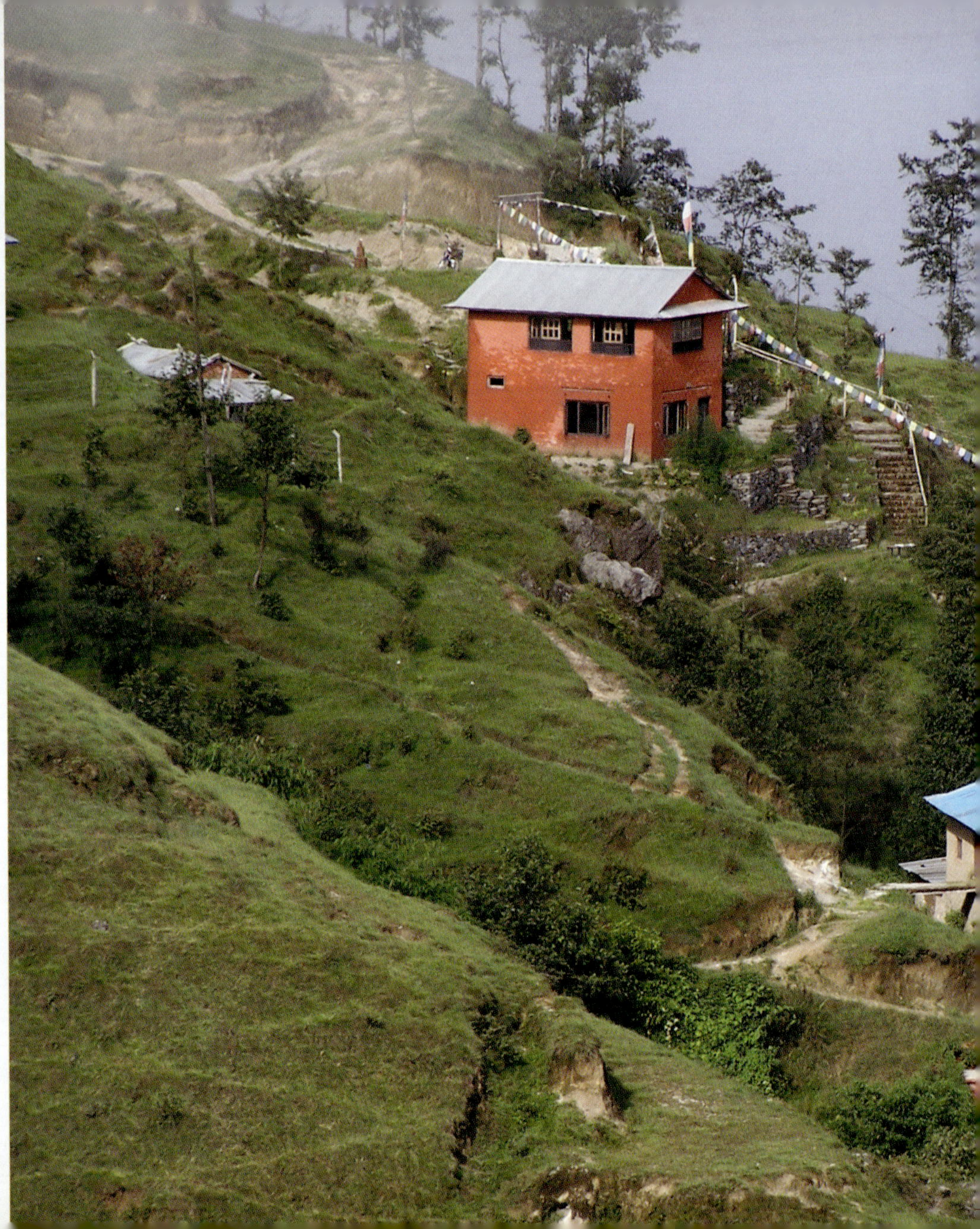

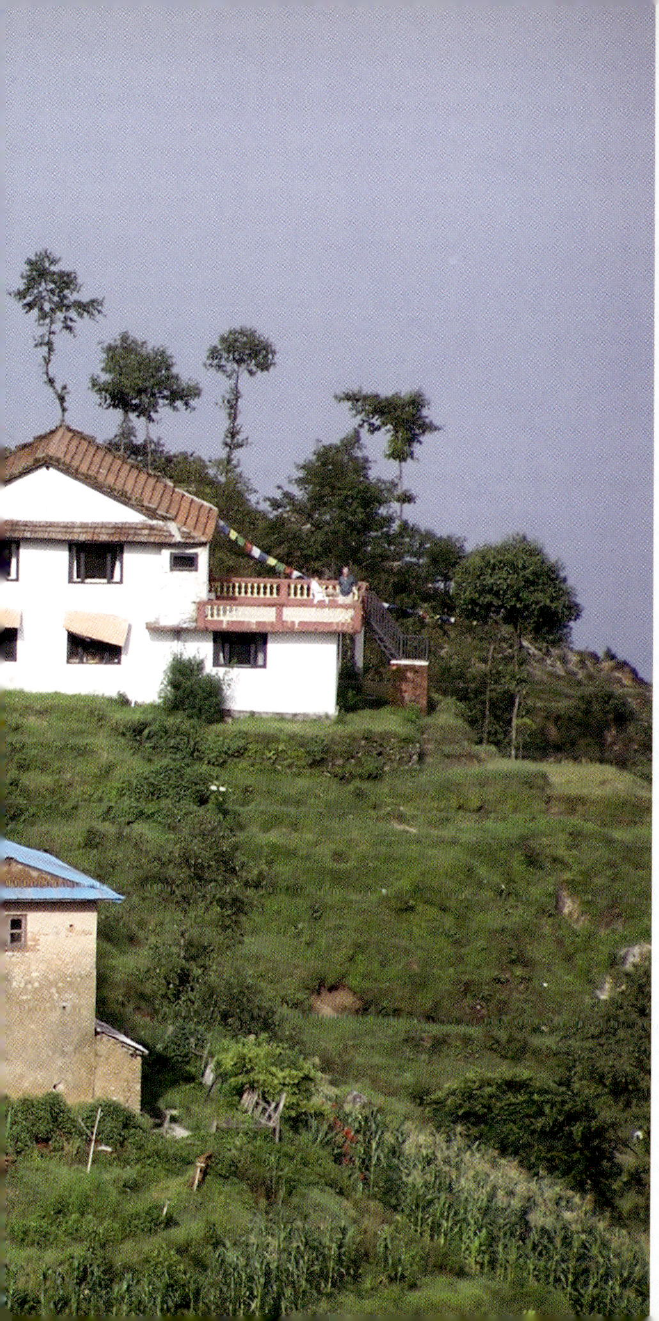

Nepal
Mountain houses and outhouses in Nagarkot.

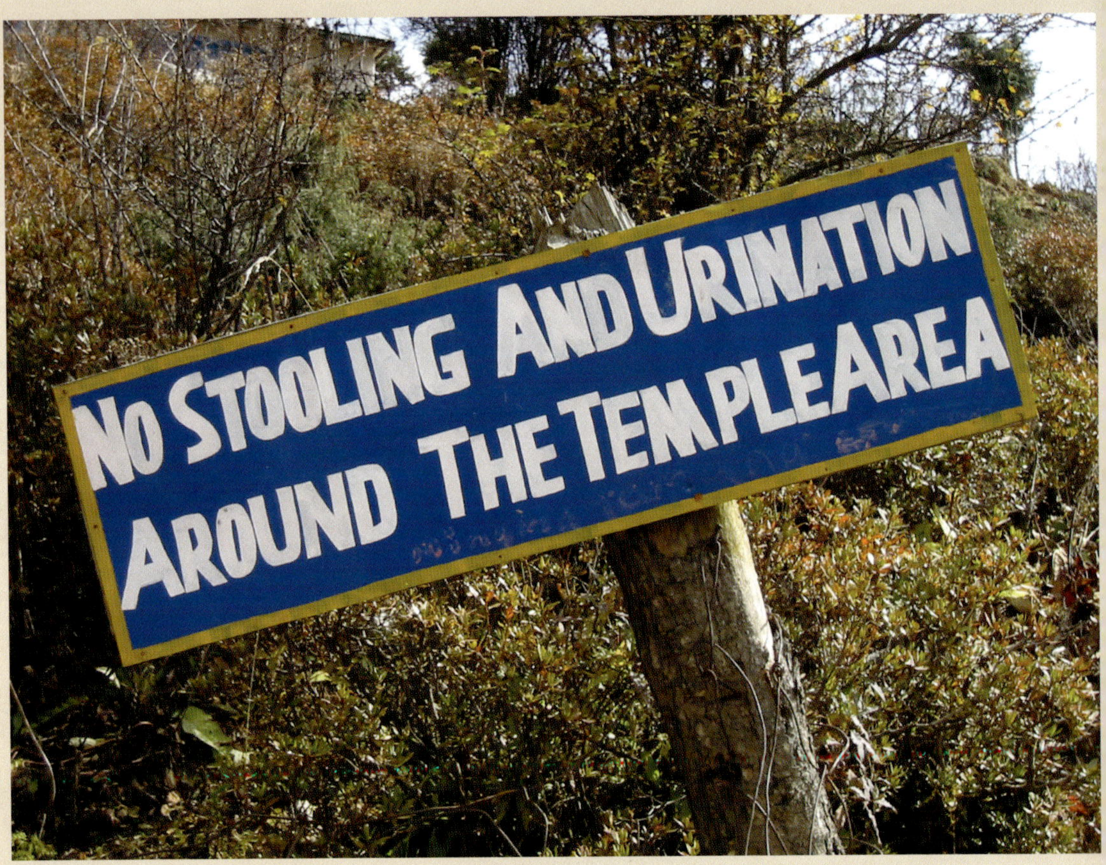

Nepal—Khumbu
Namche Bazaar region.

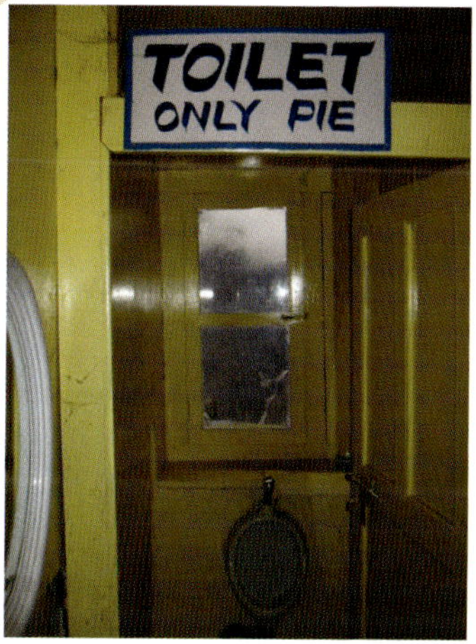

Nepal—Khumbu
Namche Bazaar region.

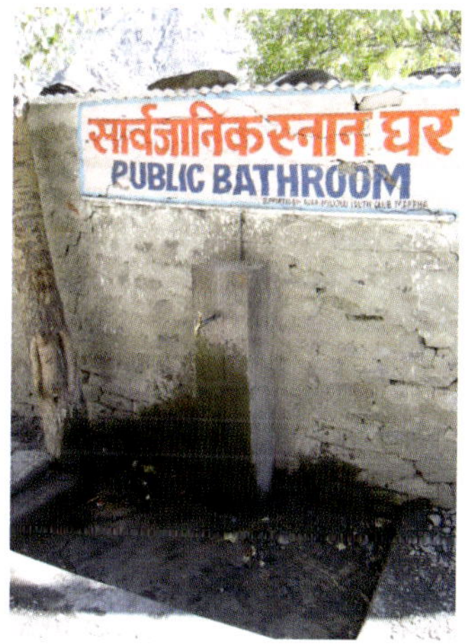

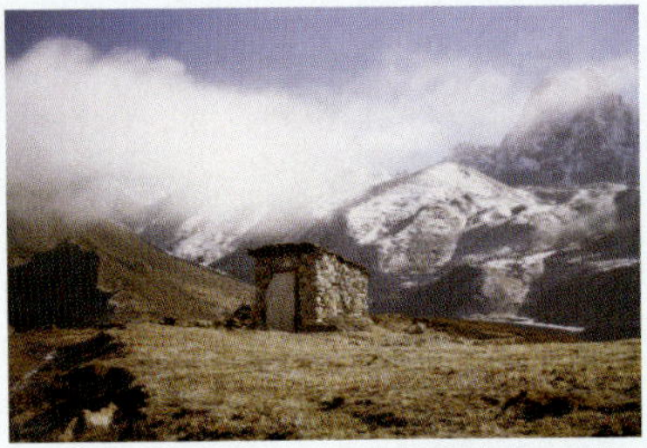

Nepal—Gokyo

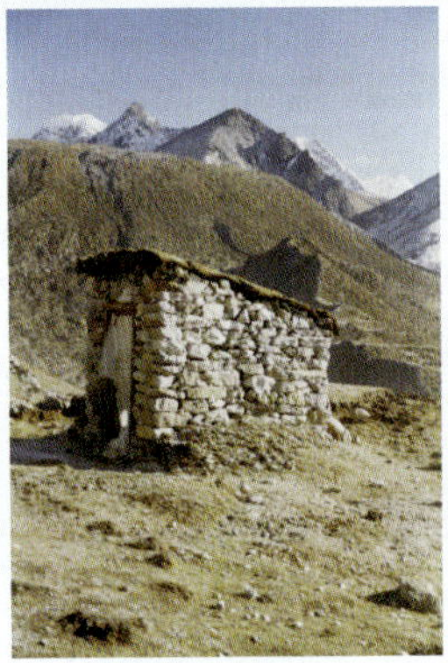

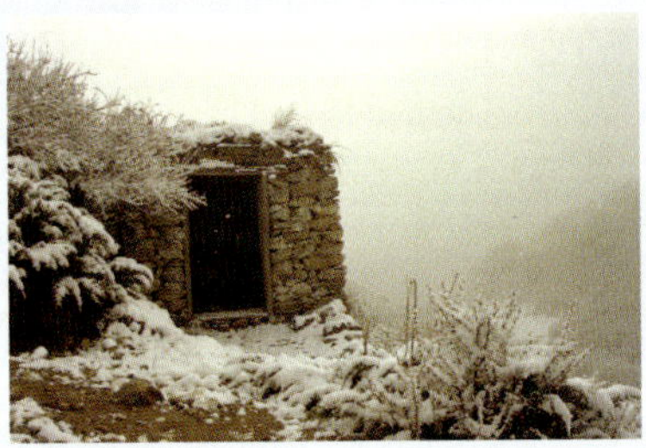

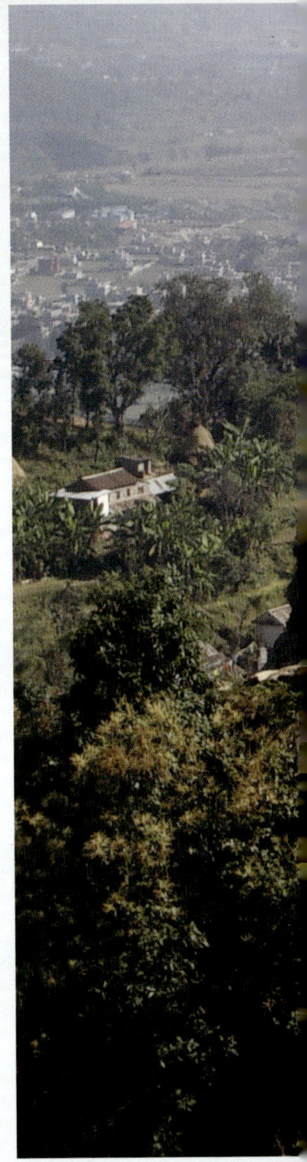

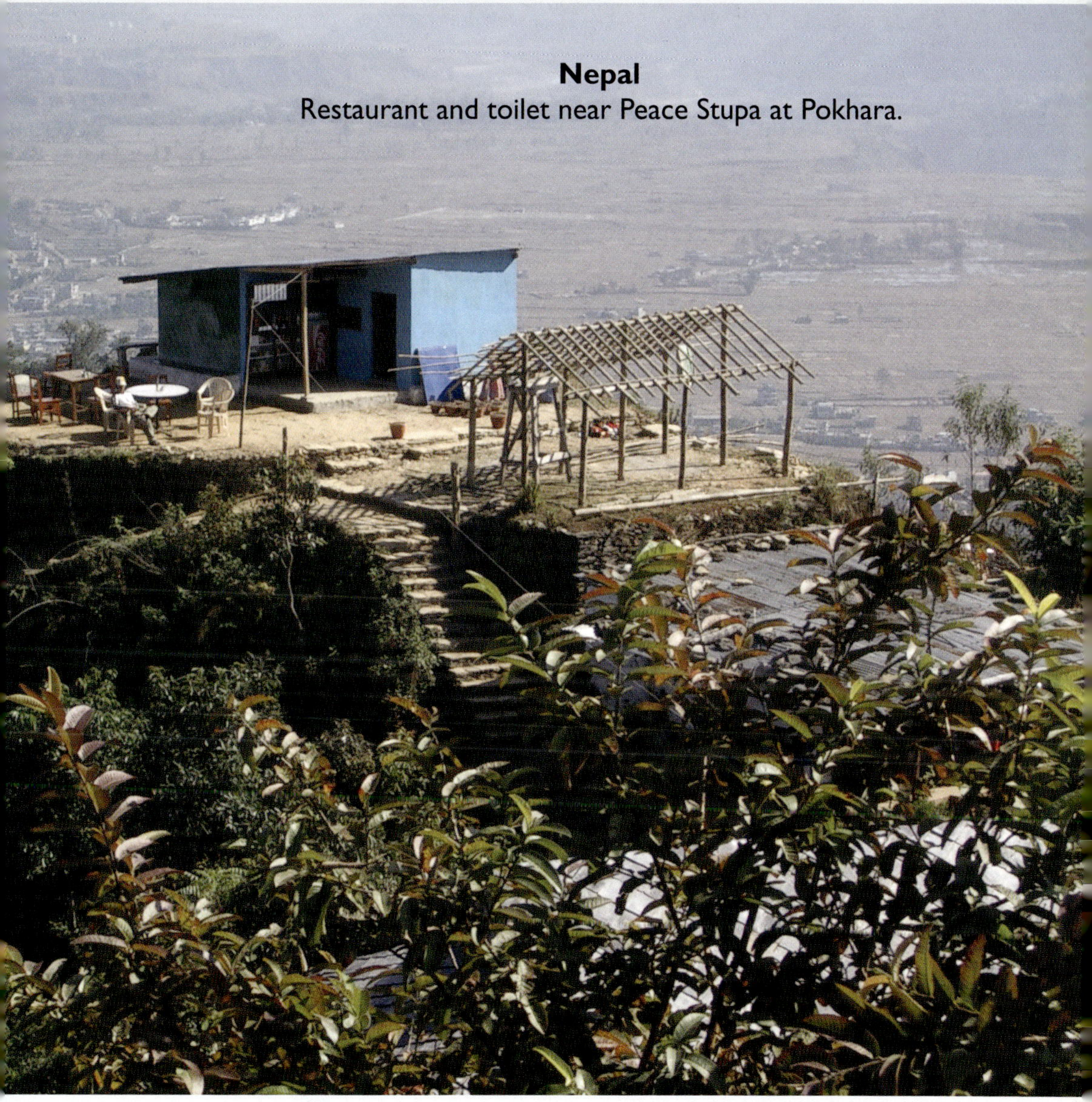

Nepal
Restaurant and toilet near Peace Stupa at Pokhara.

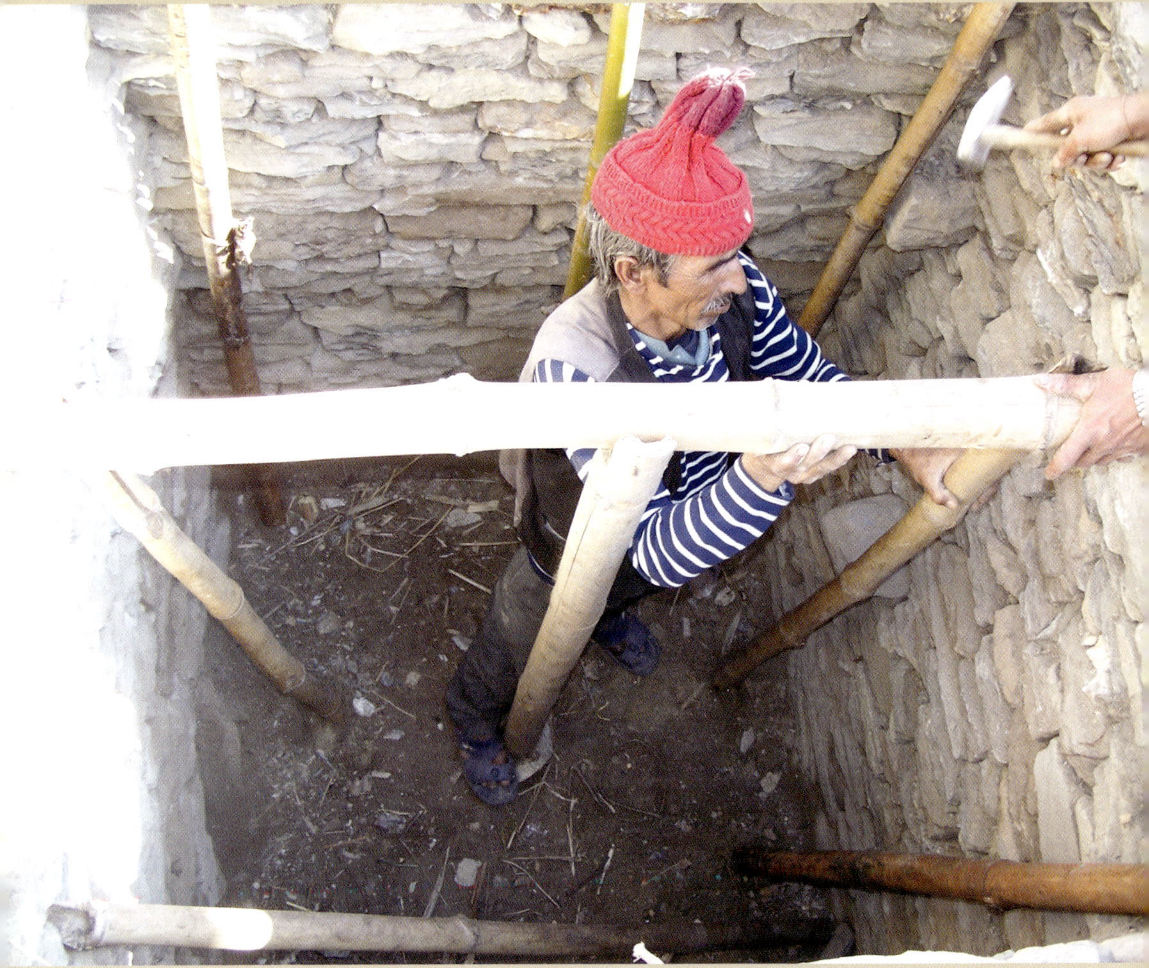

Nepal
Pit toilet in Poharepani.

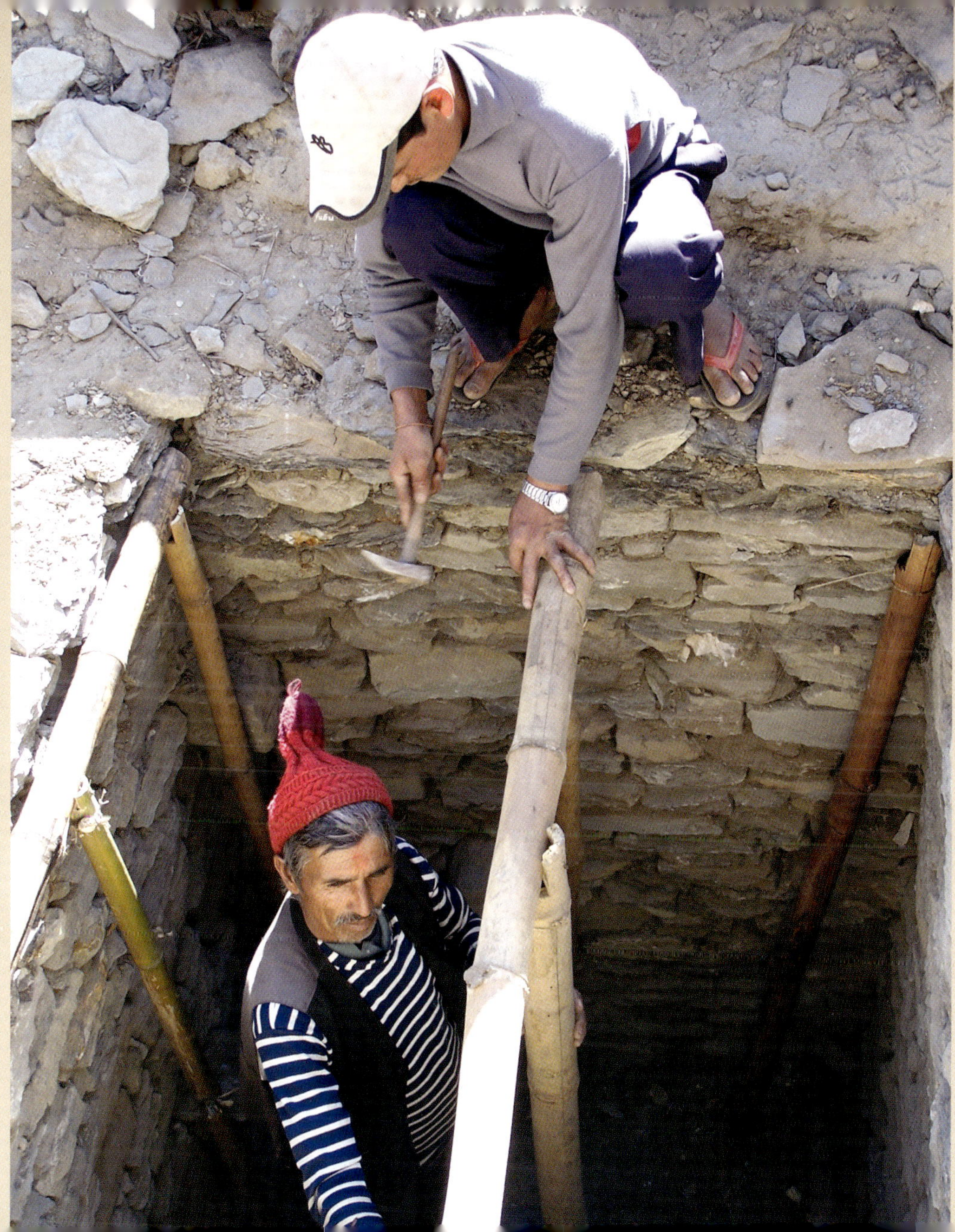

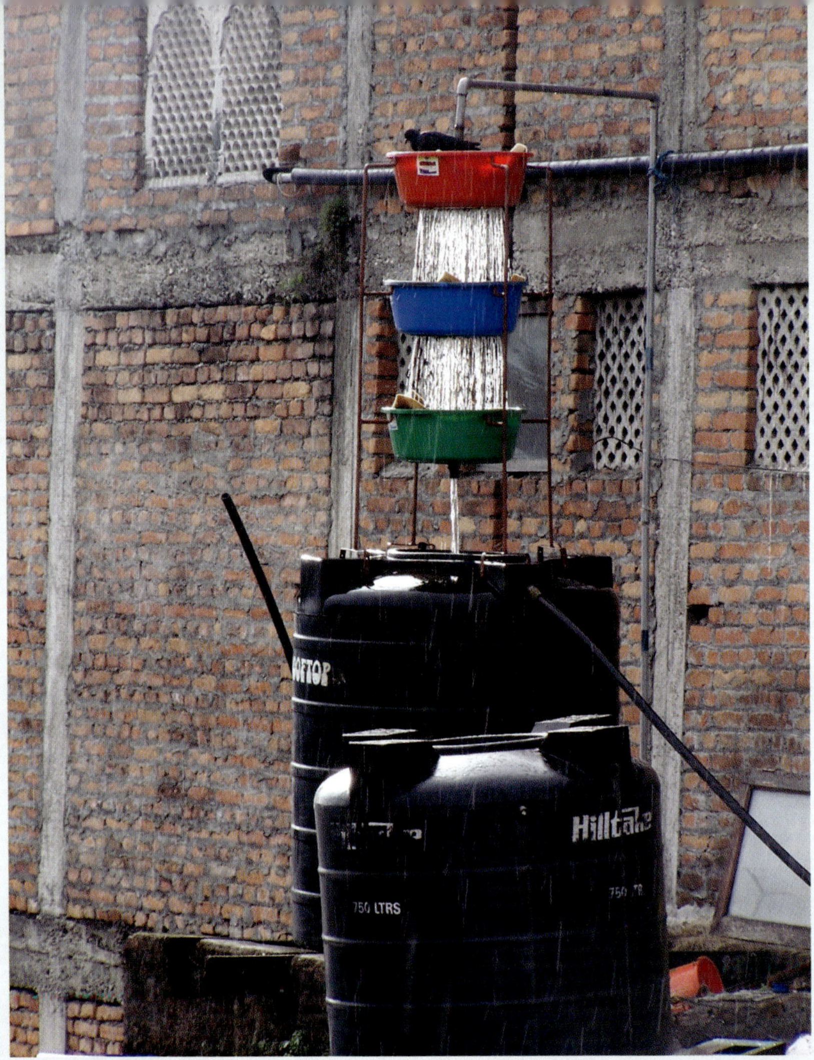

Nepal

Kathmandu rooftop water filtration. This water is good enough for flushing toilets, passable for showering but not clean enough for drinking. Note the pigeon bathing in the top basin.

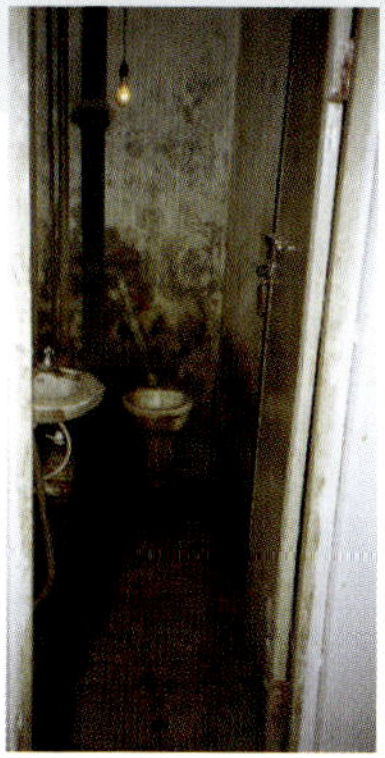

Nepal
Typical toilet.

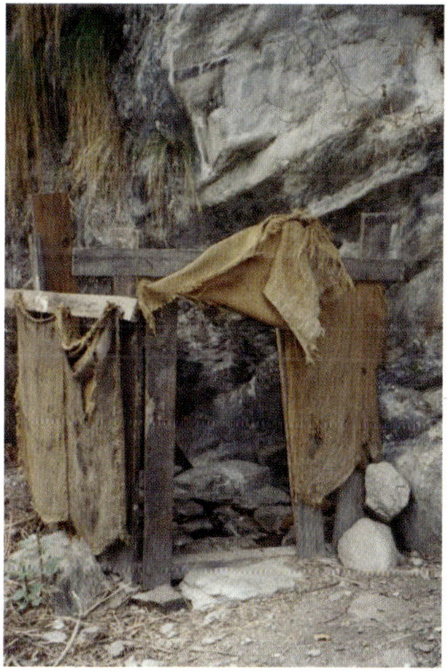

Tatopani region.

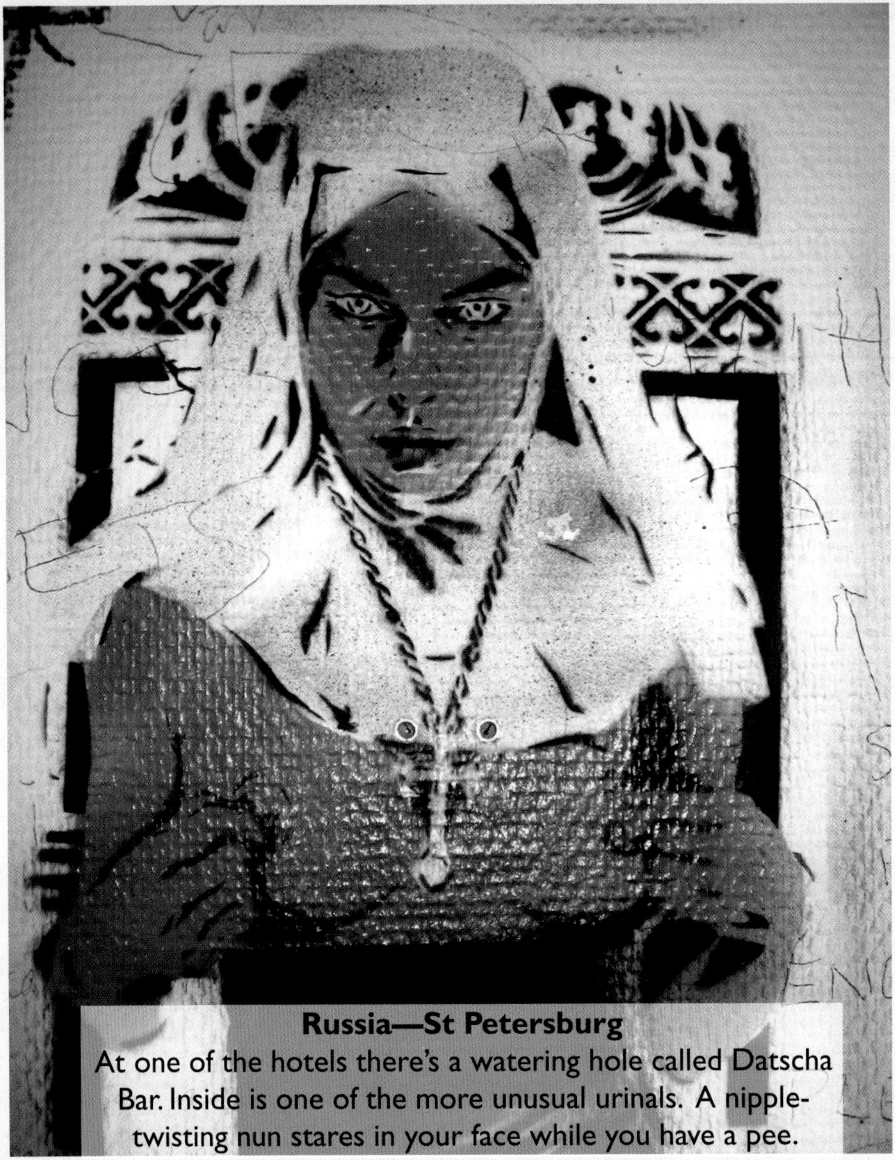

Russia—St Petersburg
At one of the hotels there's a watering hole called Datscha Bar. Inside is one of the more unusual urinals. A nipple-twisting nun stares in your face while you have a pee.

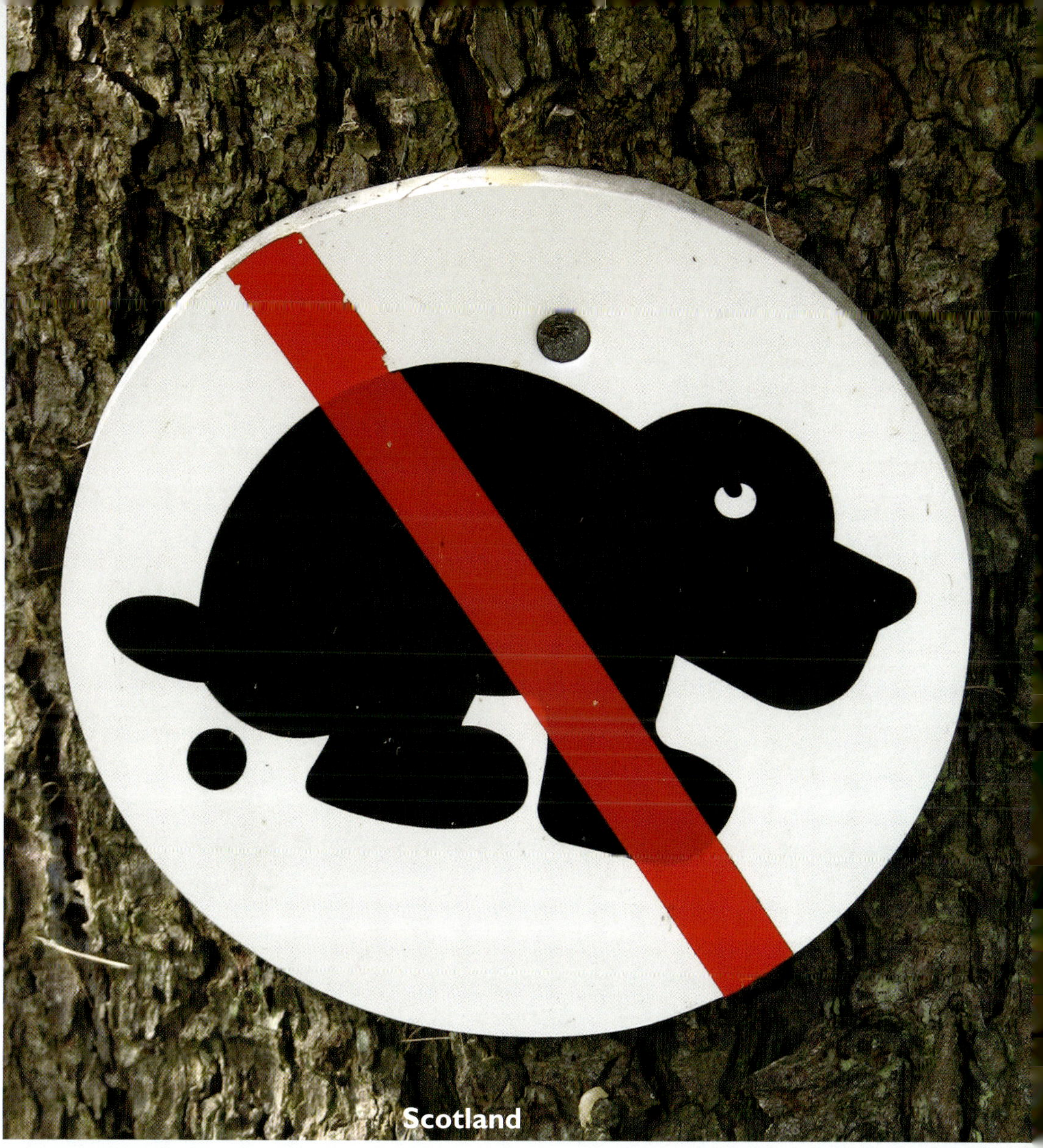

Scotland

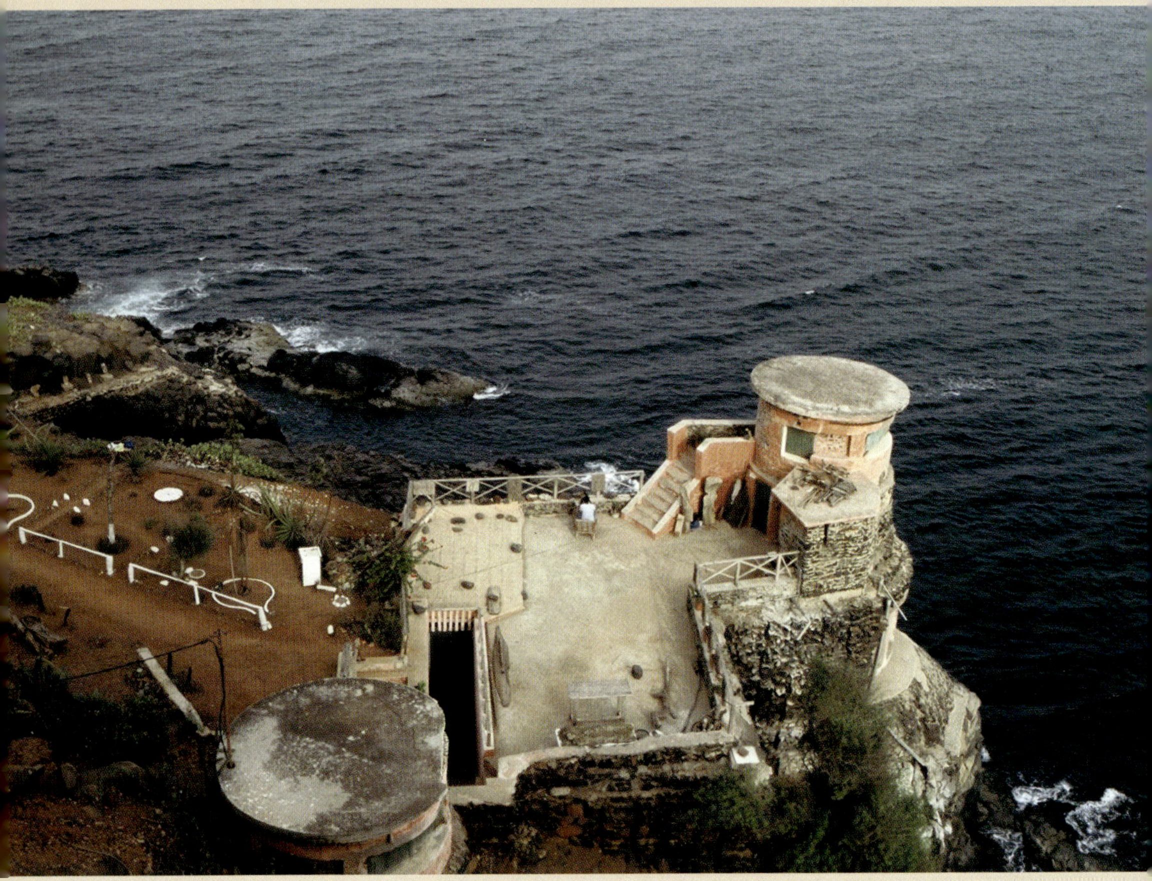

Senegal—Ille de Goree

This is an artistic community just off the Senegalese capital of Dakar. The inhabitants of the island live in the battlements and underground tunnels of the island. This photo shows one of the more prominent dwellings with the toilet to the right beneath the rubble. Note the drain further down the cliff-face. The island boasts having been the location for the cliff scenes in the film *The Guns of Navarone*.

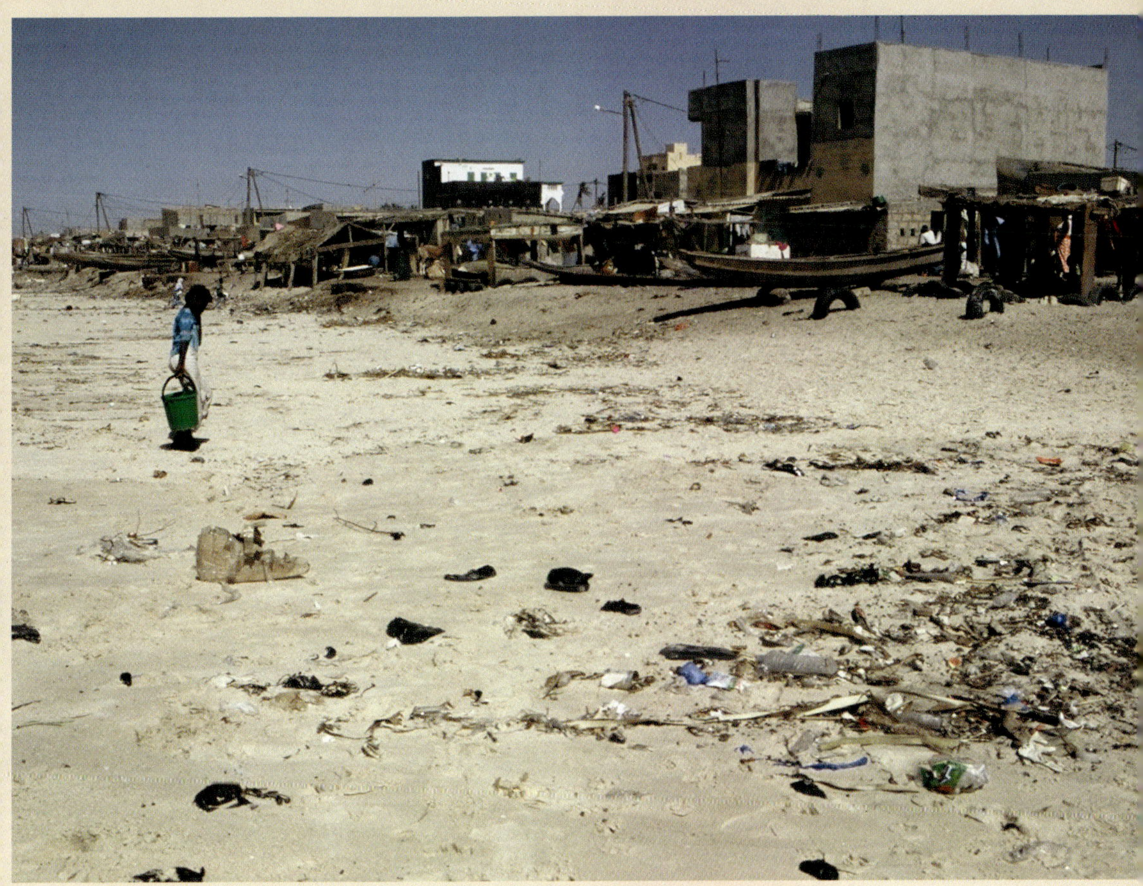

Senegal—St Louis

Some beaches are toilets. This photo shows the way a beach ends up looking if the entire area is a toilet. This is in northern Senegal in West Africa on the not-so-delightful Atlantic coast.

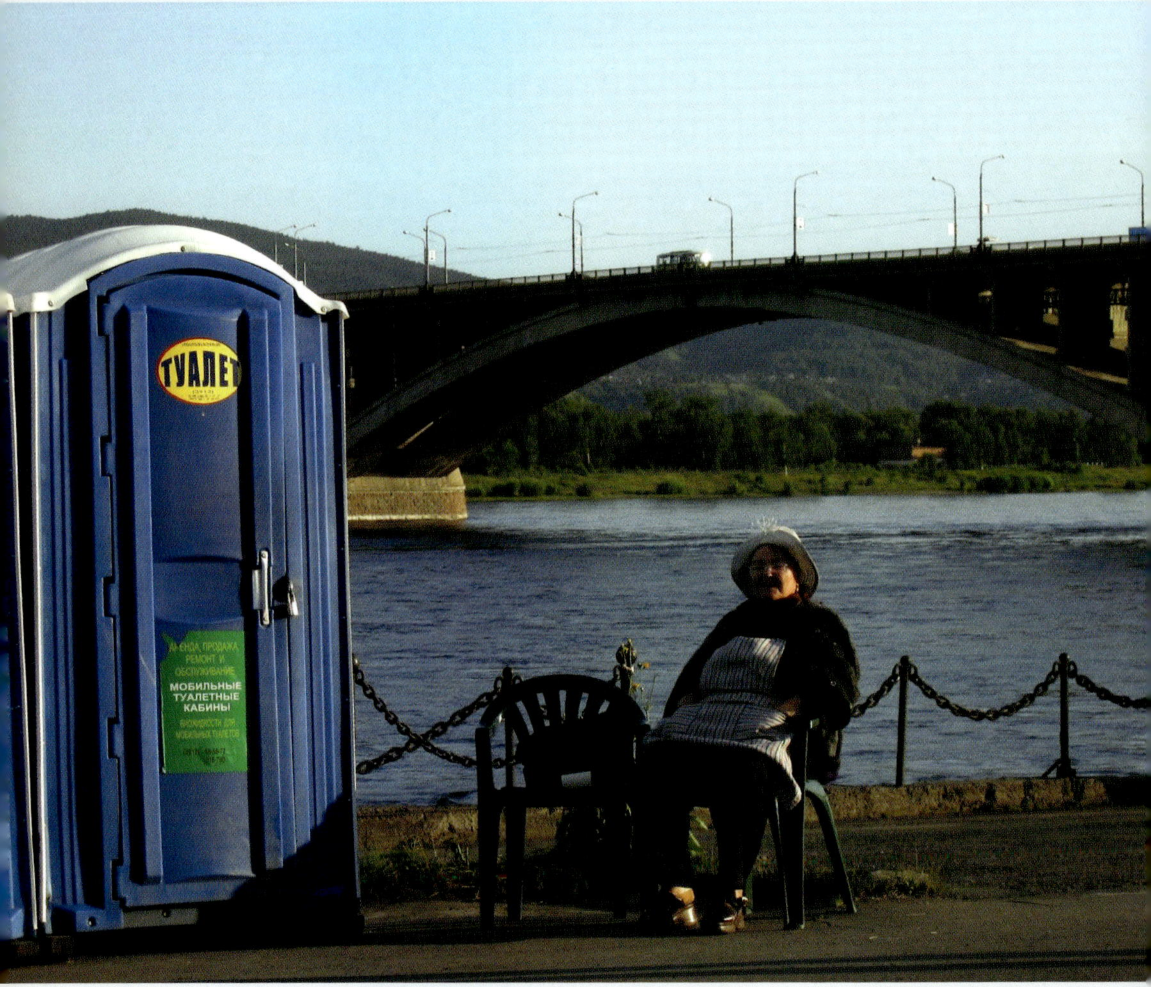

Siberia—Krasnojarsk
On the huge Yenisey River. The woman collects money and provides small amounts of toilet paper.

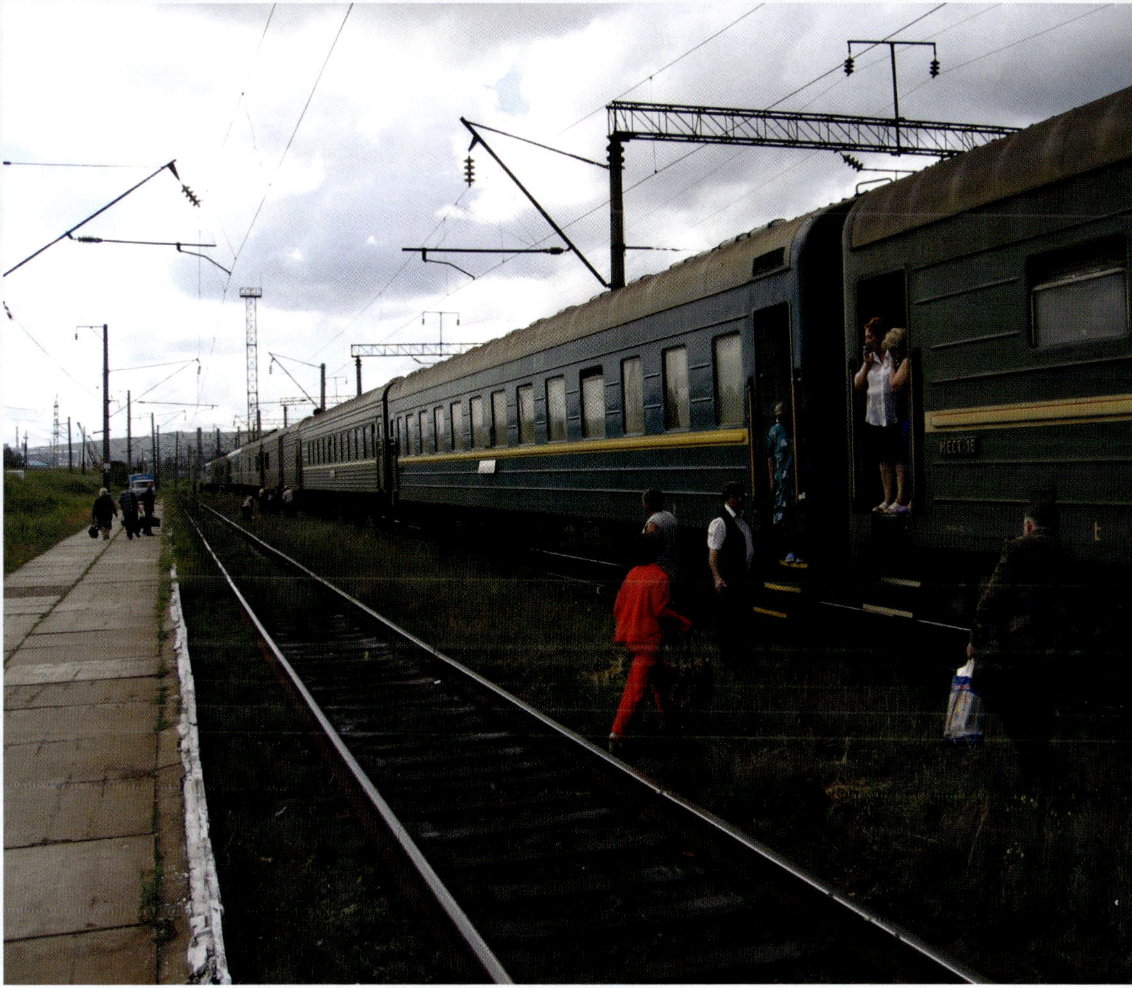

Siberia—Irkutsk Bratsk

The toilets on the train were so bad that the train stops so that passengers can use the Bratsk station toilets. Turn the page to see what greets them.

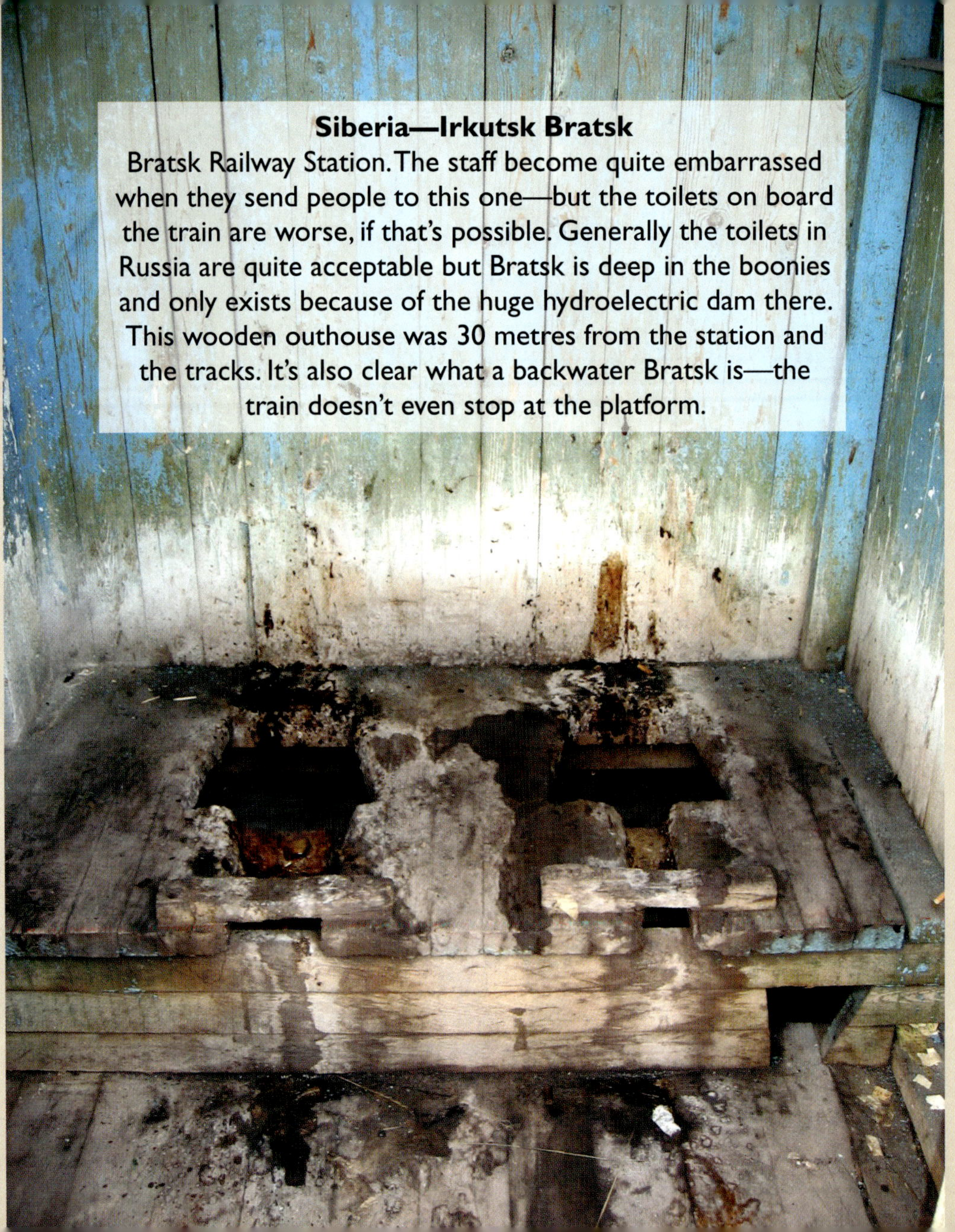

Siberia—Irkutsk Bratsk

Bratsk Railway Station. The staff become quite embarrassed when they send people to this one—but the toilets on board the train are worse, if that's possible. Generally the toilets in Russia are quite acceptable but Bratsk is deep in the boonies and only exists because of the huge hydroelectric dam there. This wooden outhouse was 30 metres from the station and the tracks. It's also clear what a backwater Bratsk is—the train doesn't even stop at the platform.

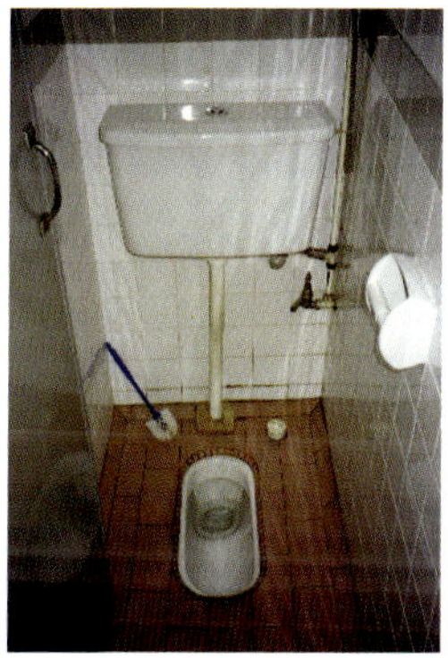

Singapore
At last, a clean one!

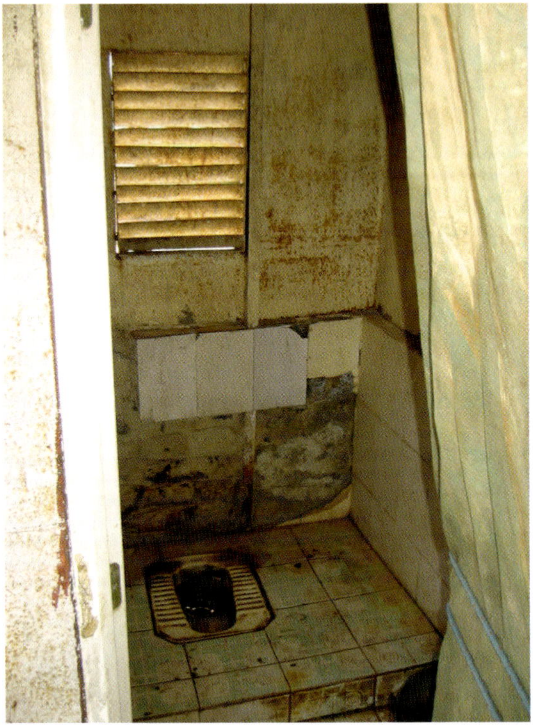

Thailand to Yunnan Route
River-boat toilet at Chiang Saen.

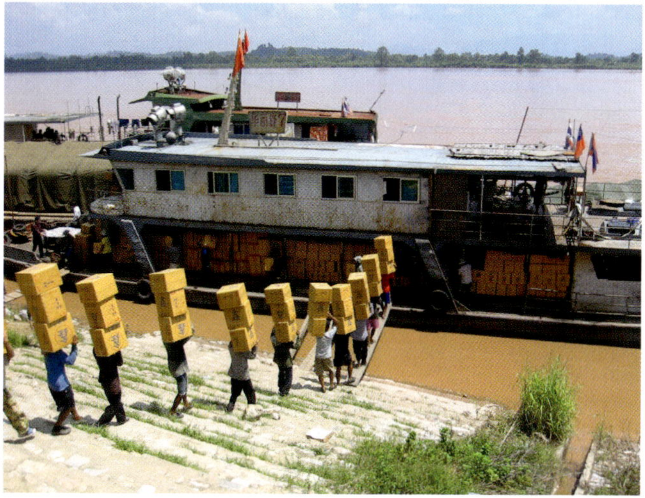

Thailand River
Boat at Chiang Saen.

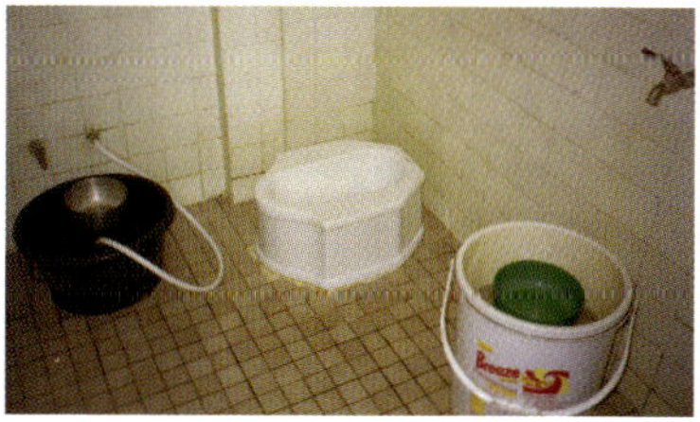

Thailand
All in one.

Thailand—Railay Beach

The thatched roof area is the loo, but sometimes, especially when the tide's out, much of the Thai coast looks like a toilet. Environmental care is often non-existent.

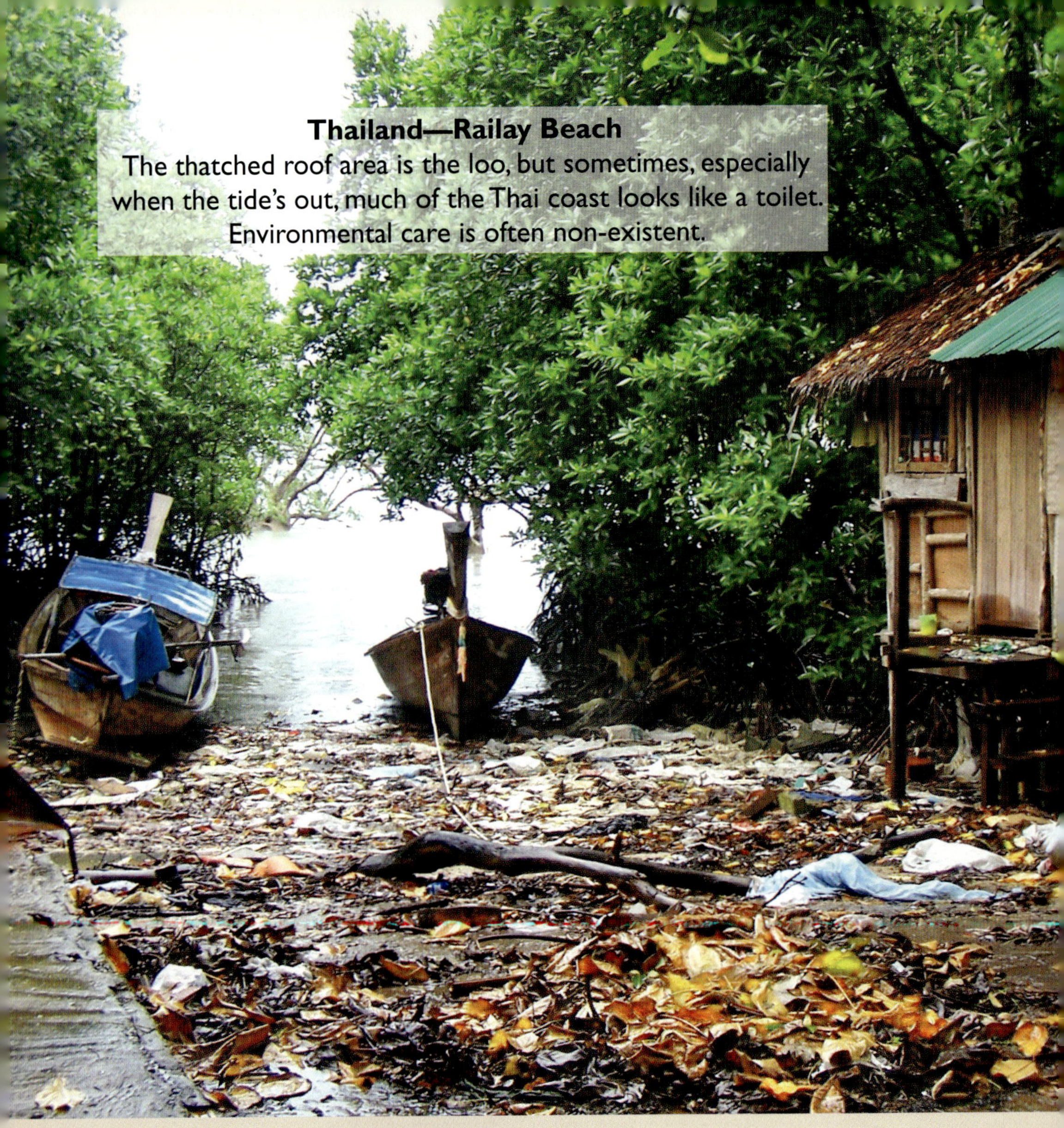

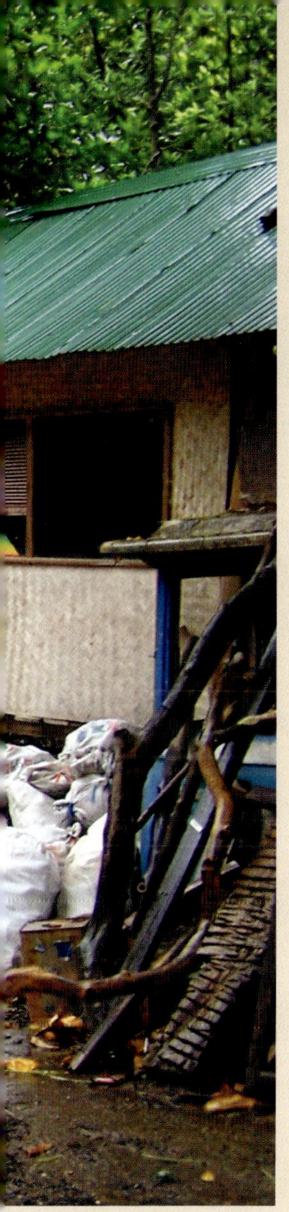

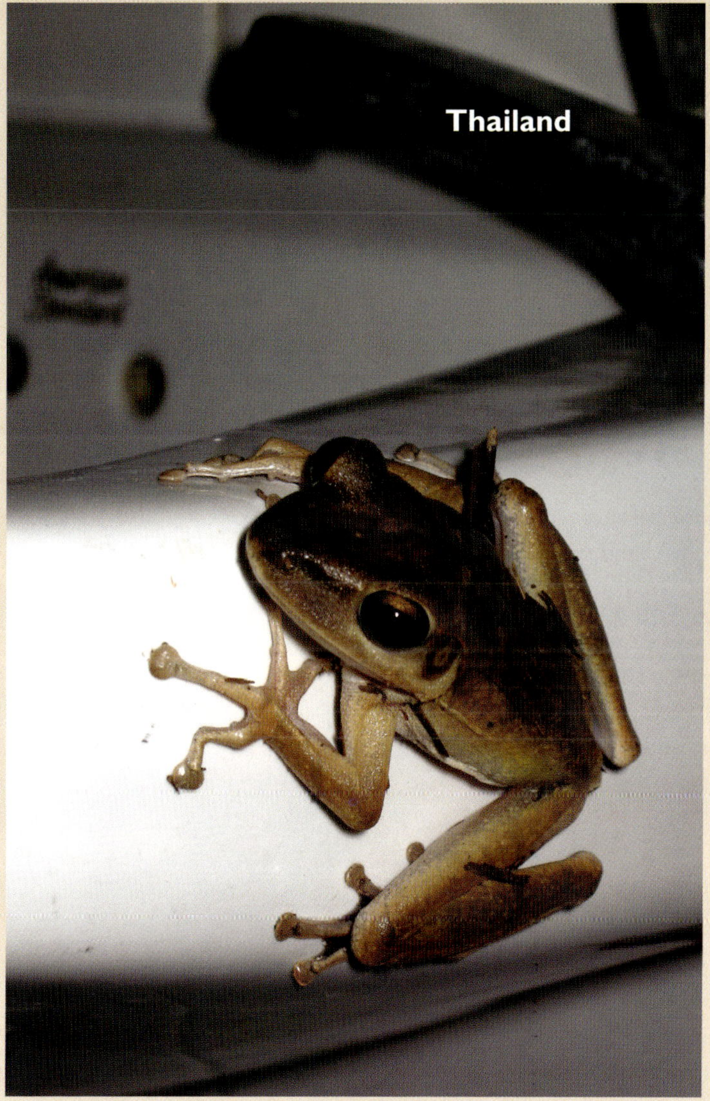

Thailand

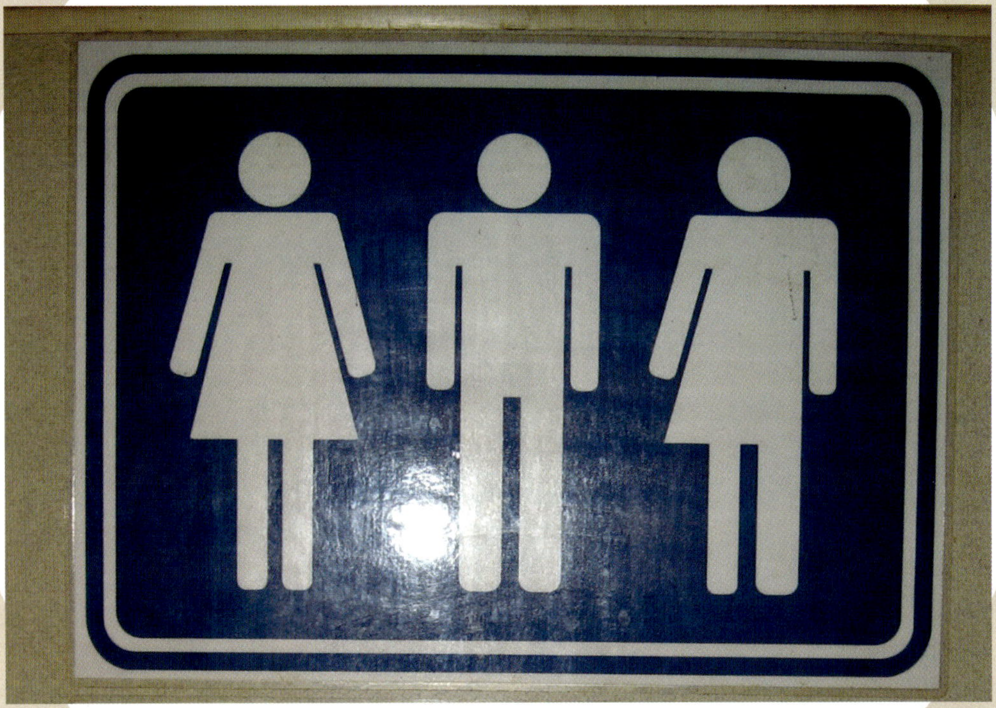

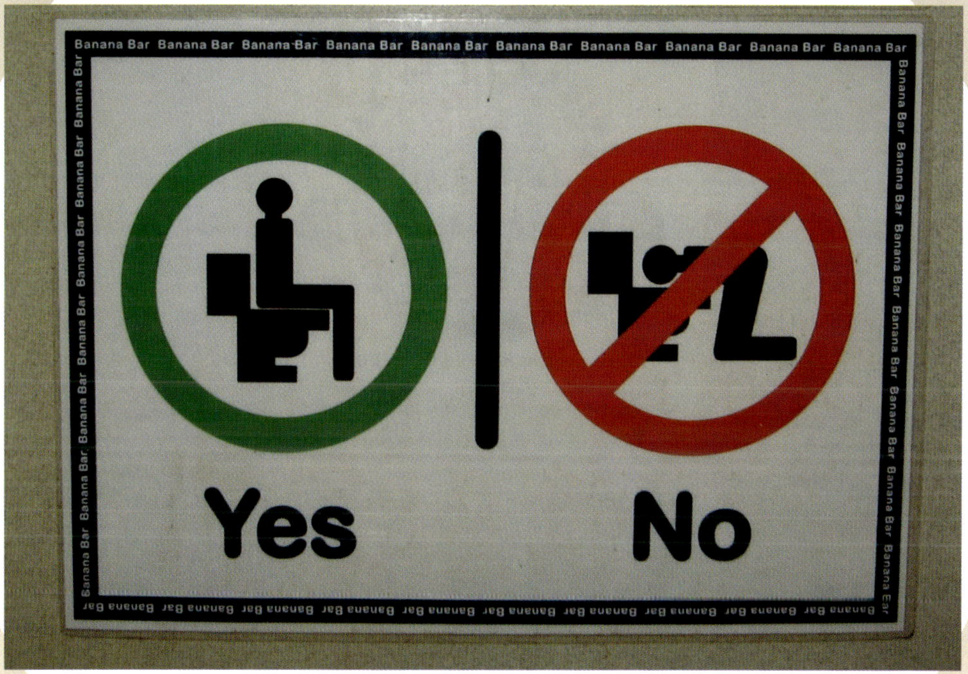
Banana Bar Banana Bar Banana Bar Banana Bar Banana Bar Banana Bar Banana Bar Banana Bar Banana Bar Banana Bar
Yes
No

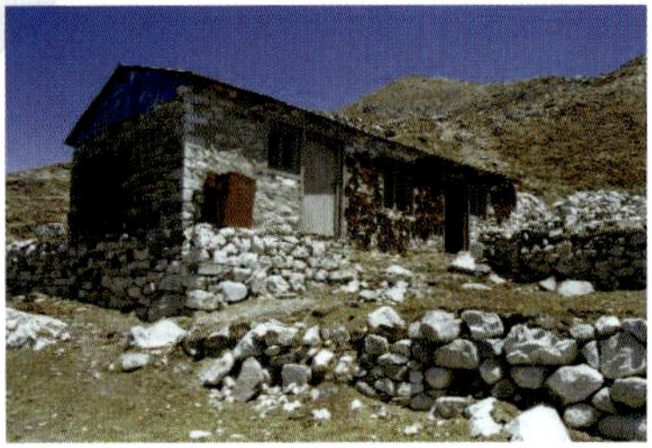

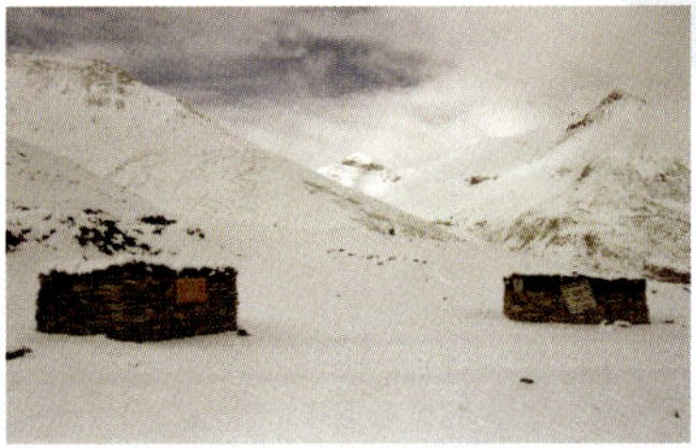

Tibet

Gokyo Trail. This is dried yak poo on a house wall on the way to the base camp of Mt Everest. Yak poo is used as the Tibetan cooking fuel.

Tibetan Plateau.

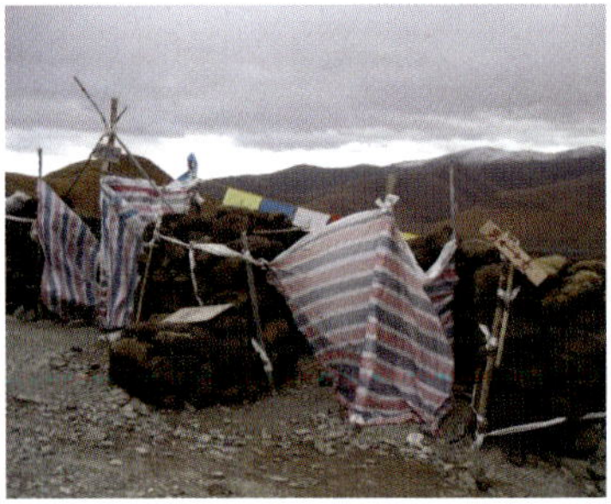

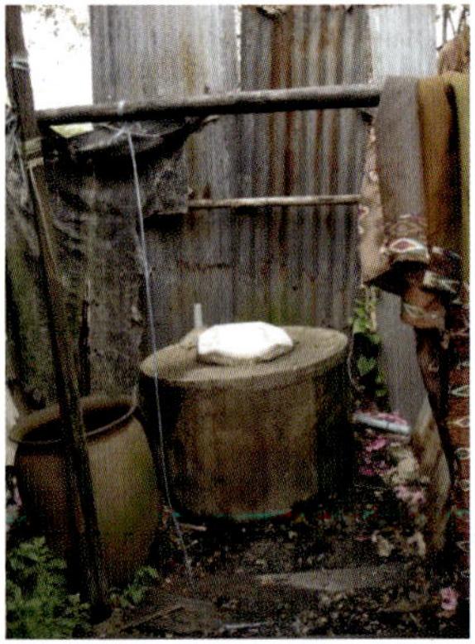

In the Tibetan hills.

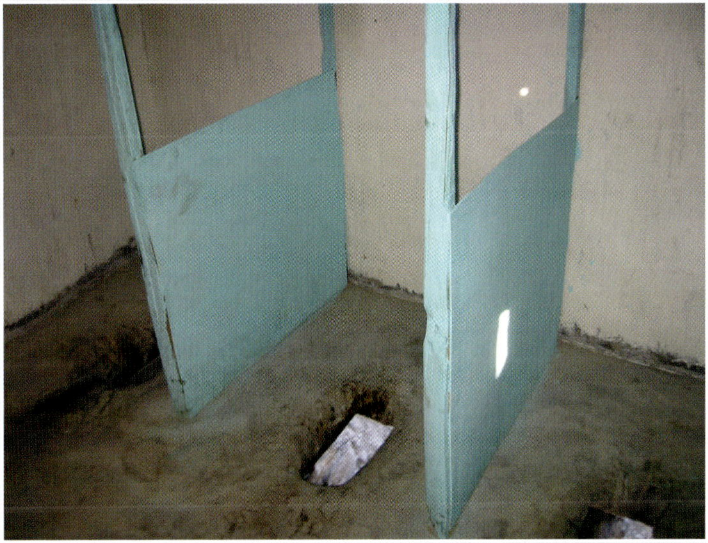

Tibet

Toilet stalls on the Nepalese border. This photo was taken near the Nepalese border. While taking a dump one hears noises from below. When you investigate, you usually discover the backside of a cow sticking out the door in the area below where you've just done your business—the animal is usually found eating the paper of the people who have just wiped their arses!

It makes you think twice before you order beef in Tibet!

In some parts of the world, such as India, pigs are often seen guzzling at sewer pipes ready for whatever comes through as soon as they see a human heading for the loo.

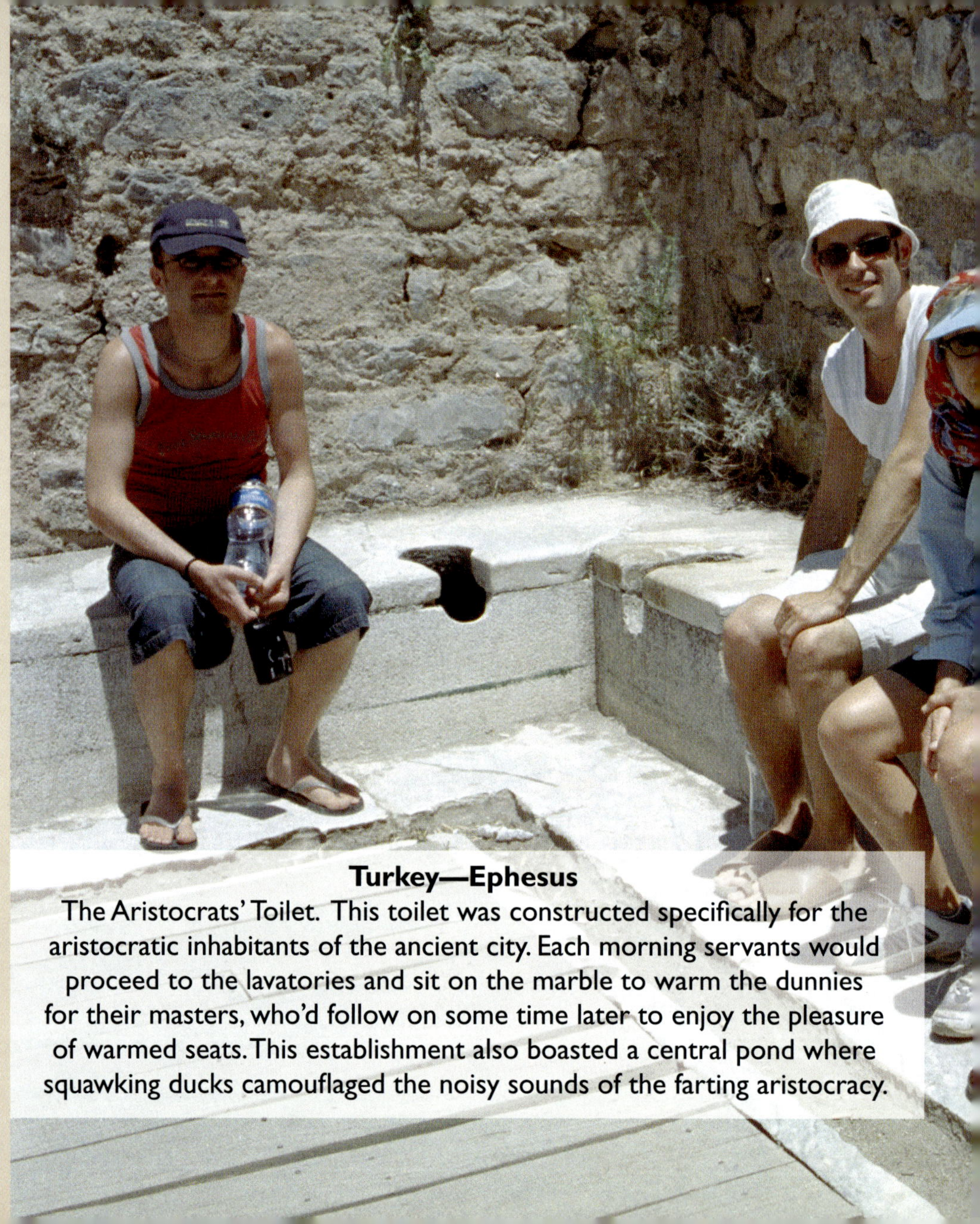

Turkey—Ephesus

The Aristocrats' Toilet. This toilet was constructed specifically for the aristocratic inhabitants of the ancient city. Each morning servants would proceed to the lavatories and sit on the marble to warm the dunnies for their masters, who'd follow on some time later to enjoy the pleasure of warmed seats. This establishment also boasted a central pond where squawking ducks camouflaged the noisy sounds of the farting aristocracy.

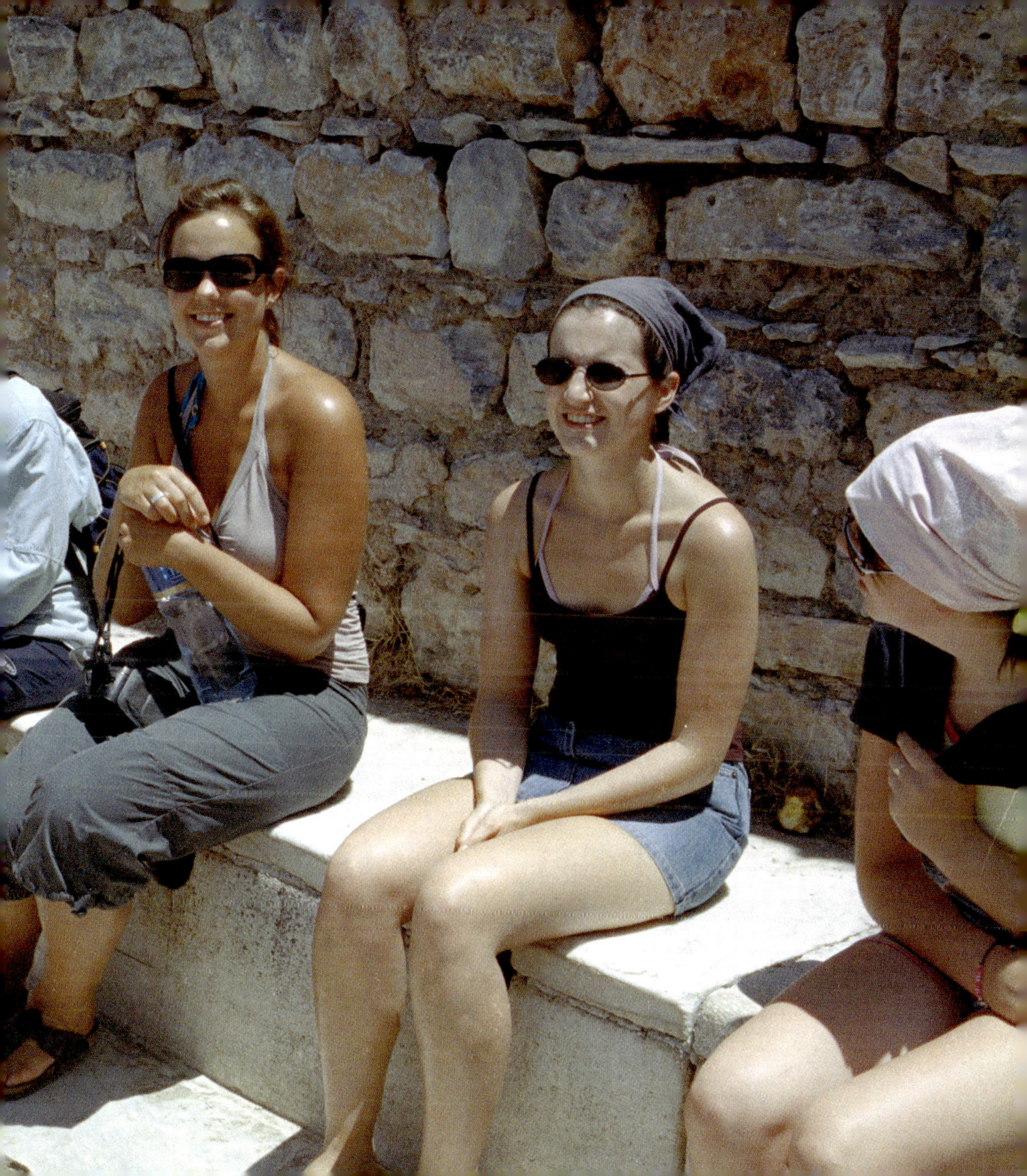

Zambia—
Zambezi River

Only metres from the shores of the Zambezi River, this bathroom boasts steaming hot water, fresh handtowels daily and the entire area is swept and raked every morning. The photo was taken at Jungle Junction Bovu Island, a civilised camp beside the river, about an hour's drive through the bush from Livingstone but only 15 minutes by boat from Victoria Falls, or as the local Lozi people call it, Mosi-Oa-Tunya, 'the smoke that thunders'.

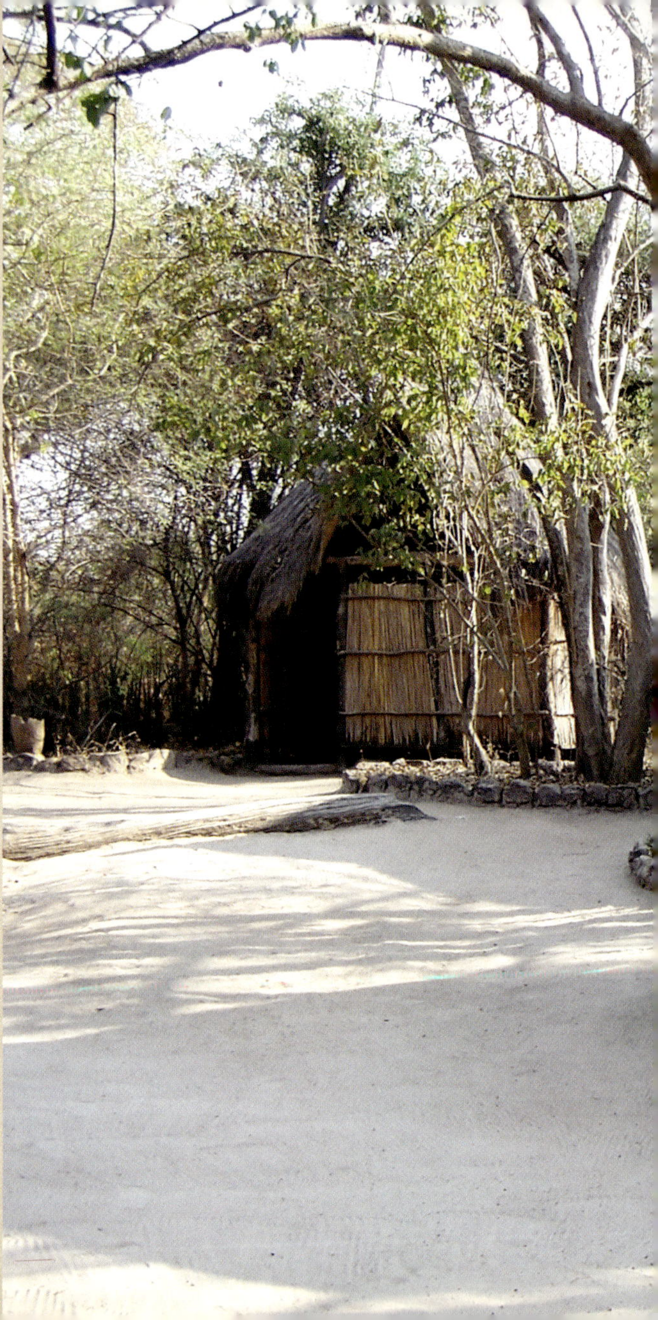

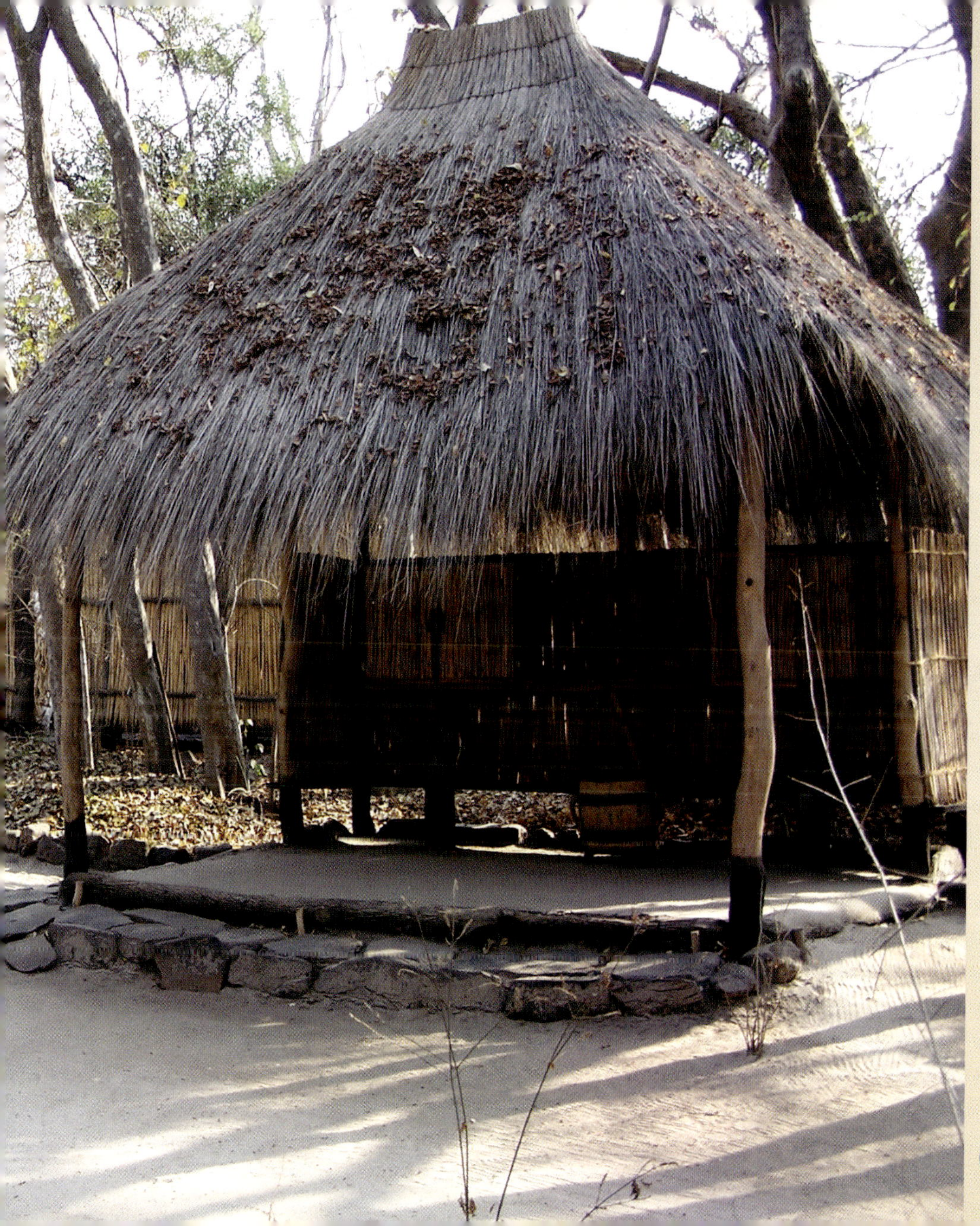

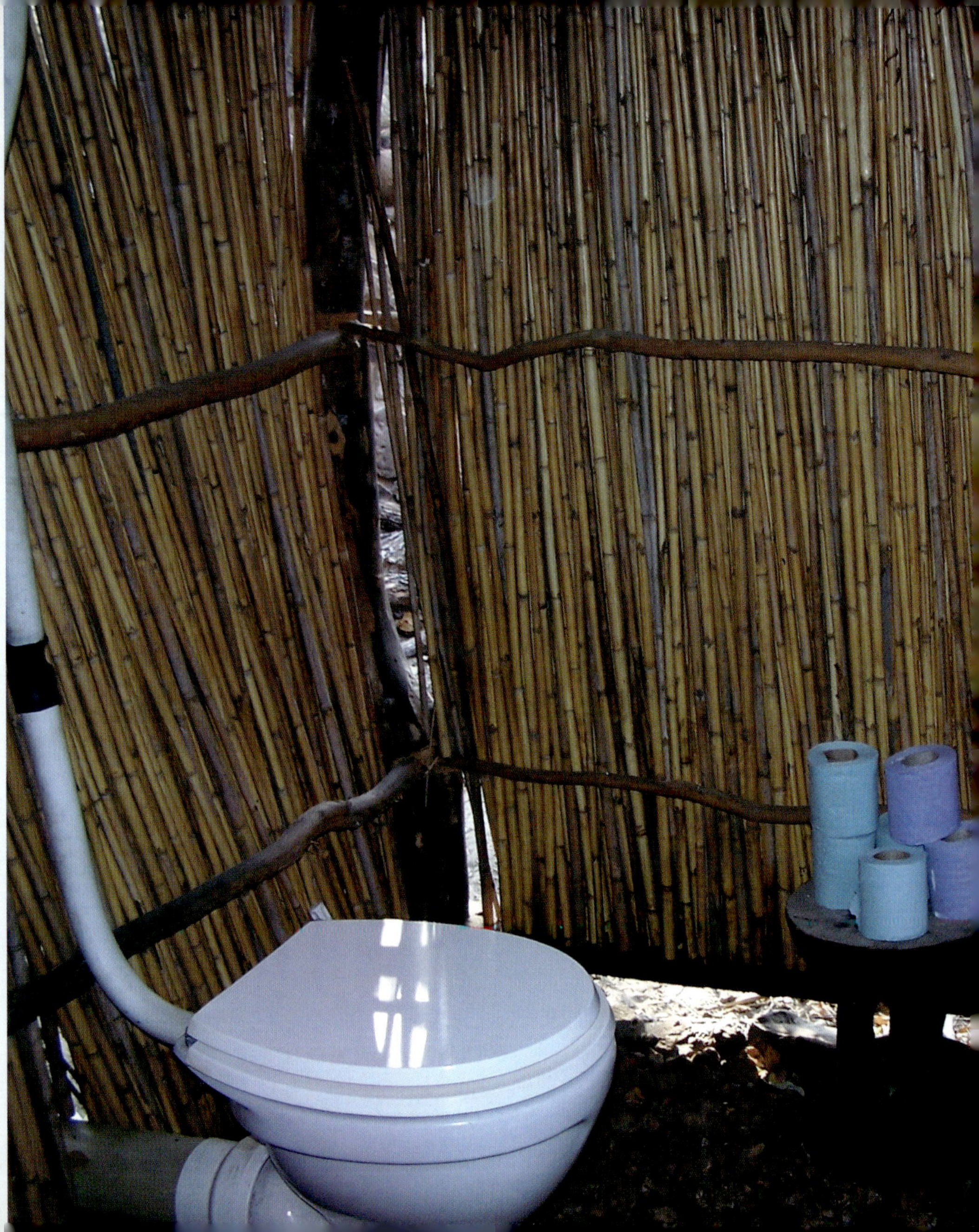

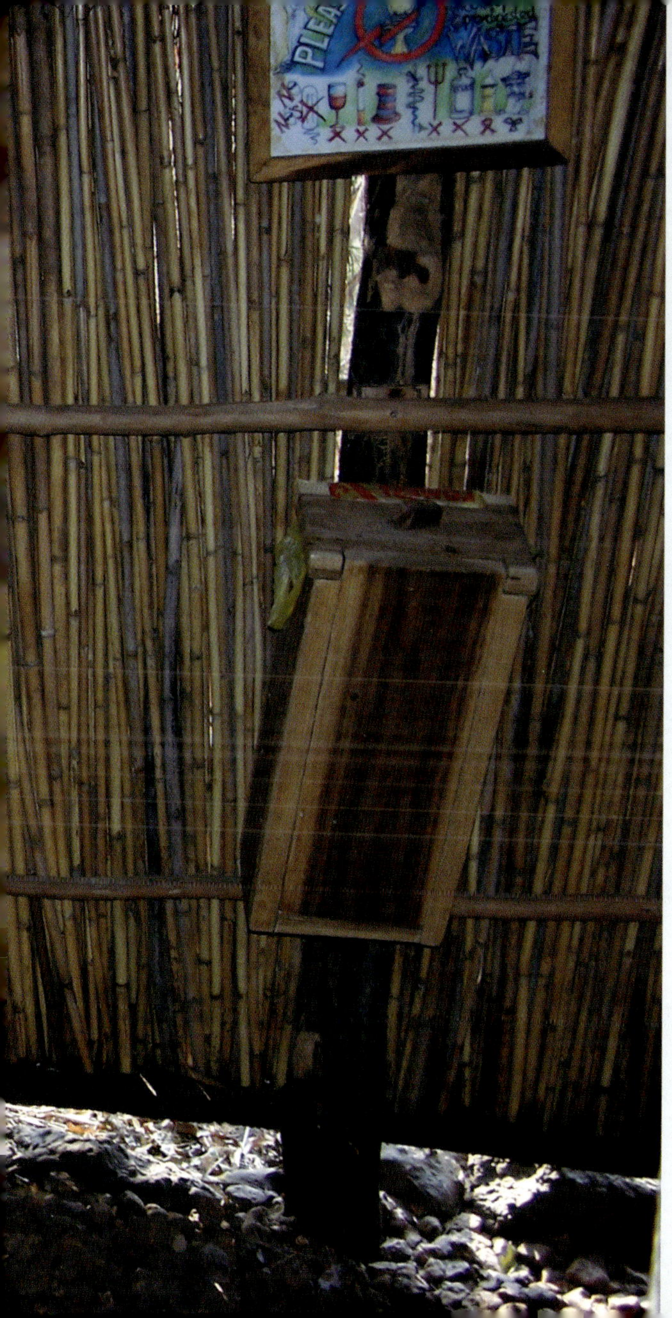

Zambia—Zambezi River

The flush toilet had an abundance of toilet paper available and was a real luxury. At night, hurricane lamps were lit outside on the pathways leading to the toilets in case the odd crocodile wandered in. It's much better to see one than not, they believe.

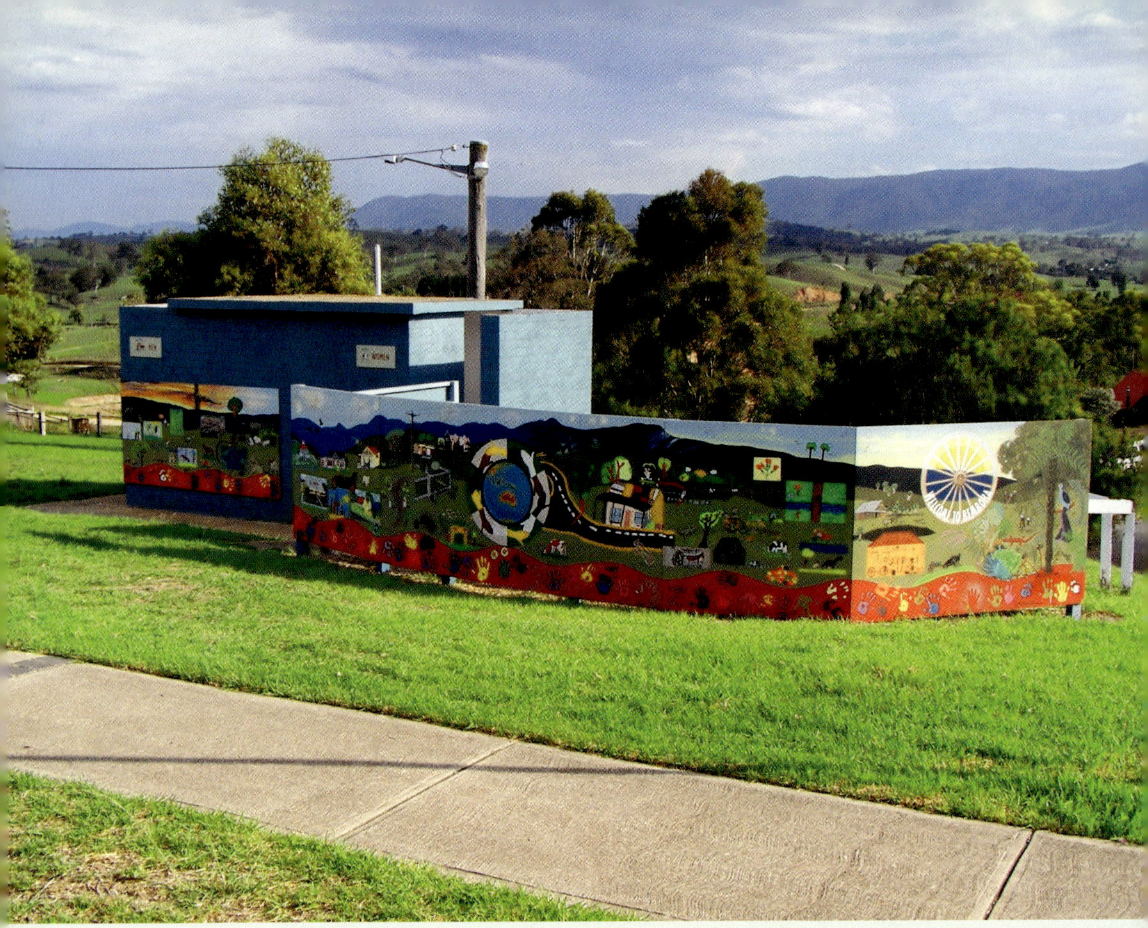

Australia—Bemboka, NSW

Bemboka was originally known as Colombo but was re-named in 1883. Today it boasts an artistic community, evidence of which can be seen in the art around the town. It is also a notable timber town with many of the town's buildings made from timber.

Australia—Bega, NSW

Port-a-loos have recently been made famous by the award-winning film *Kenny*. This one is the standard RTA model for use by road workers caught short while on the job.

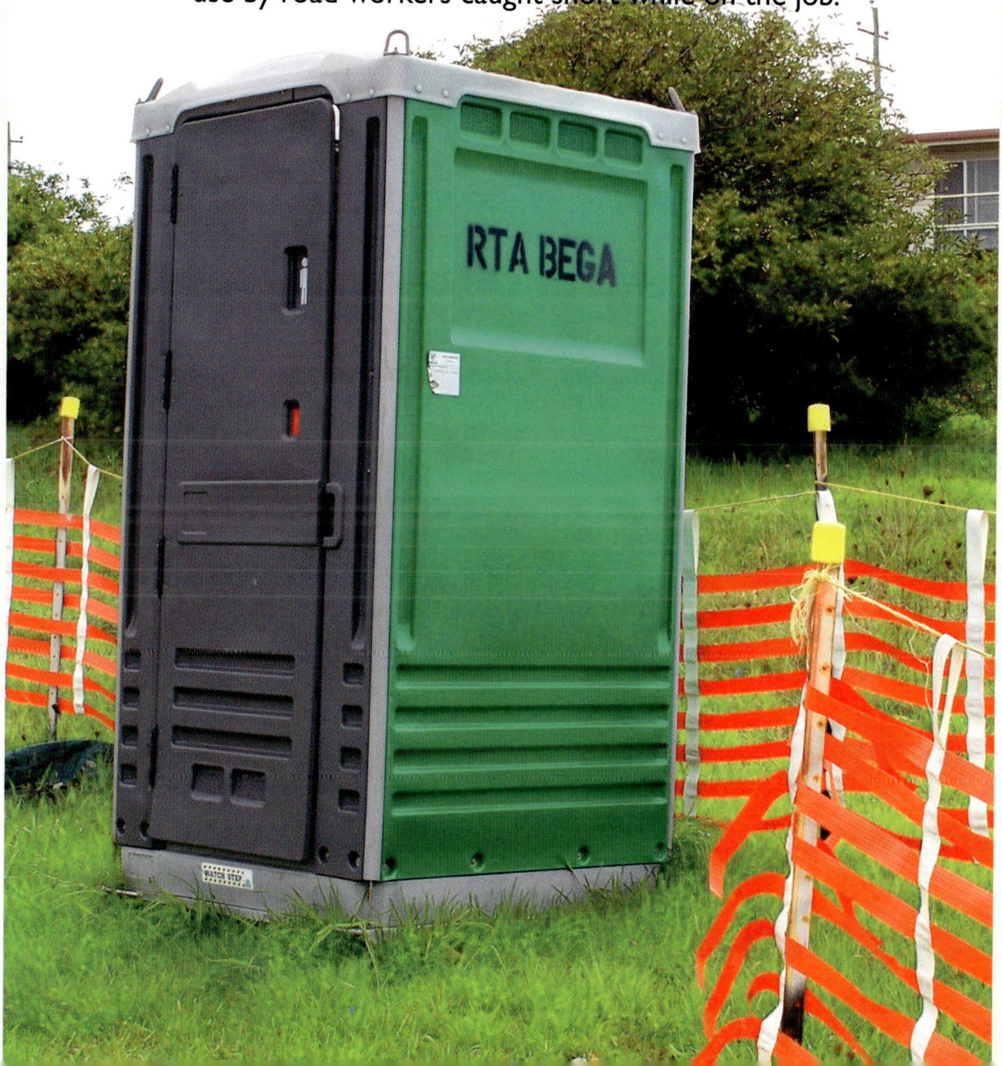

Australia—Boydtown, NSW

This contemporary gents' toilet design is located in a very upmarket B&B in southern NSW.

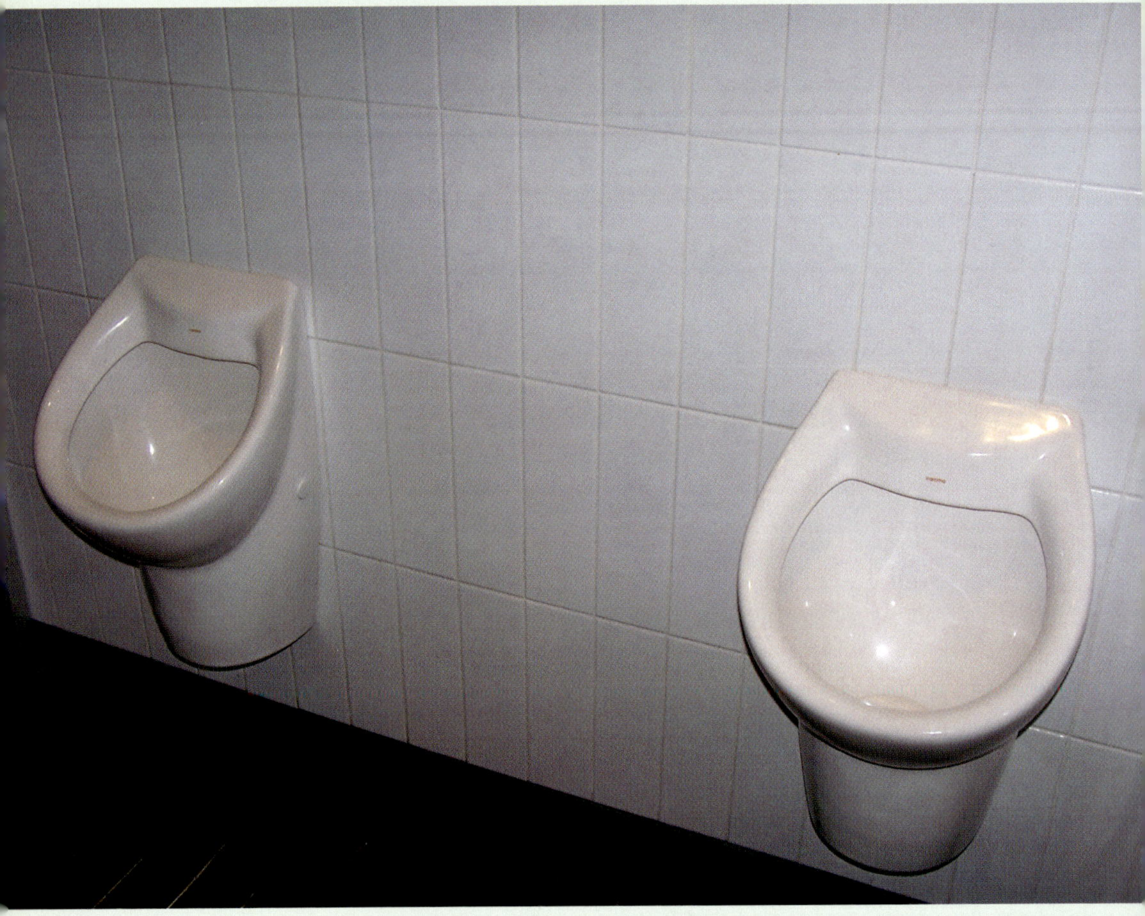

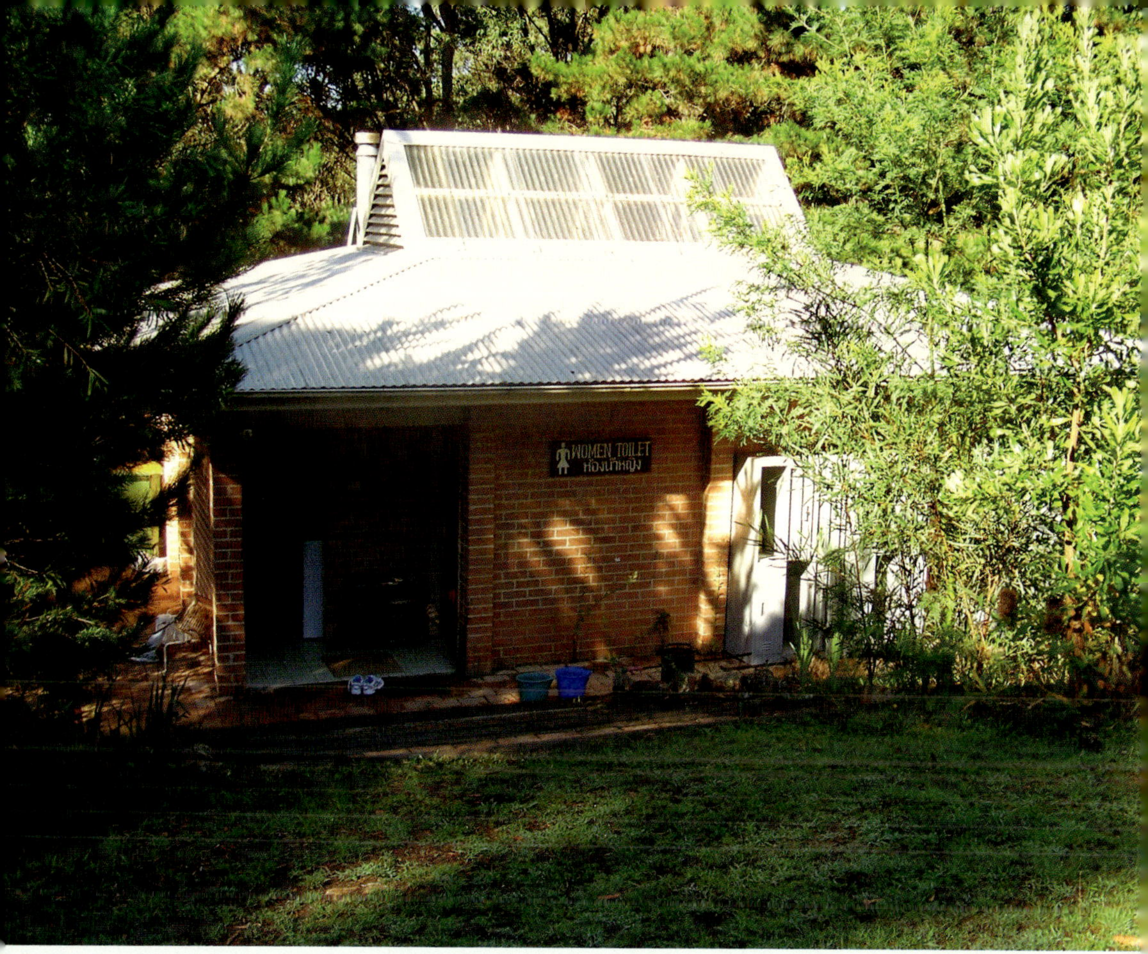

Australia—Bundanoon, NSW

This is the women's toilet block at Sunnataram Buddhist Monastery. Established in 1990, the monastery sits on 100 acres of tranquil bushland, and houses a small community of monks who follow the ascetic Thai forest tradition. The sandstone temple on the site is beautiful.

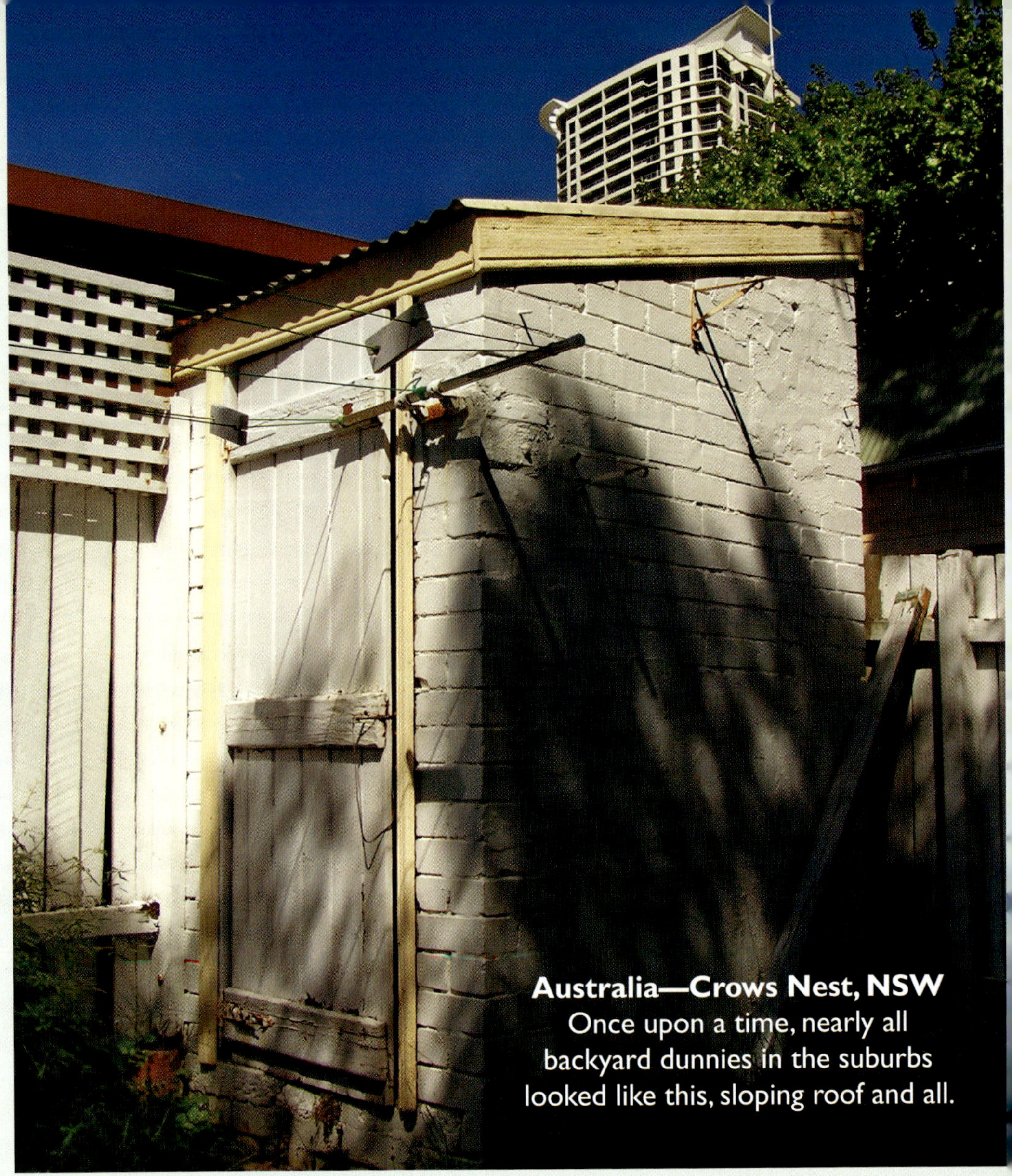

Australia—Crows Nest, NSW
Once upon a time, nearly all backyard dunnies in the suburbs looked like this, sloping roof and all.

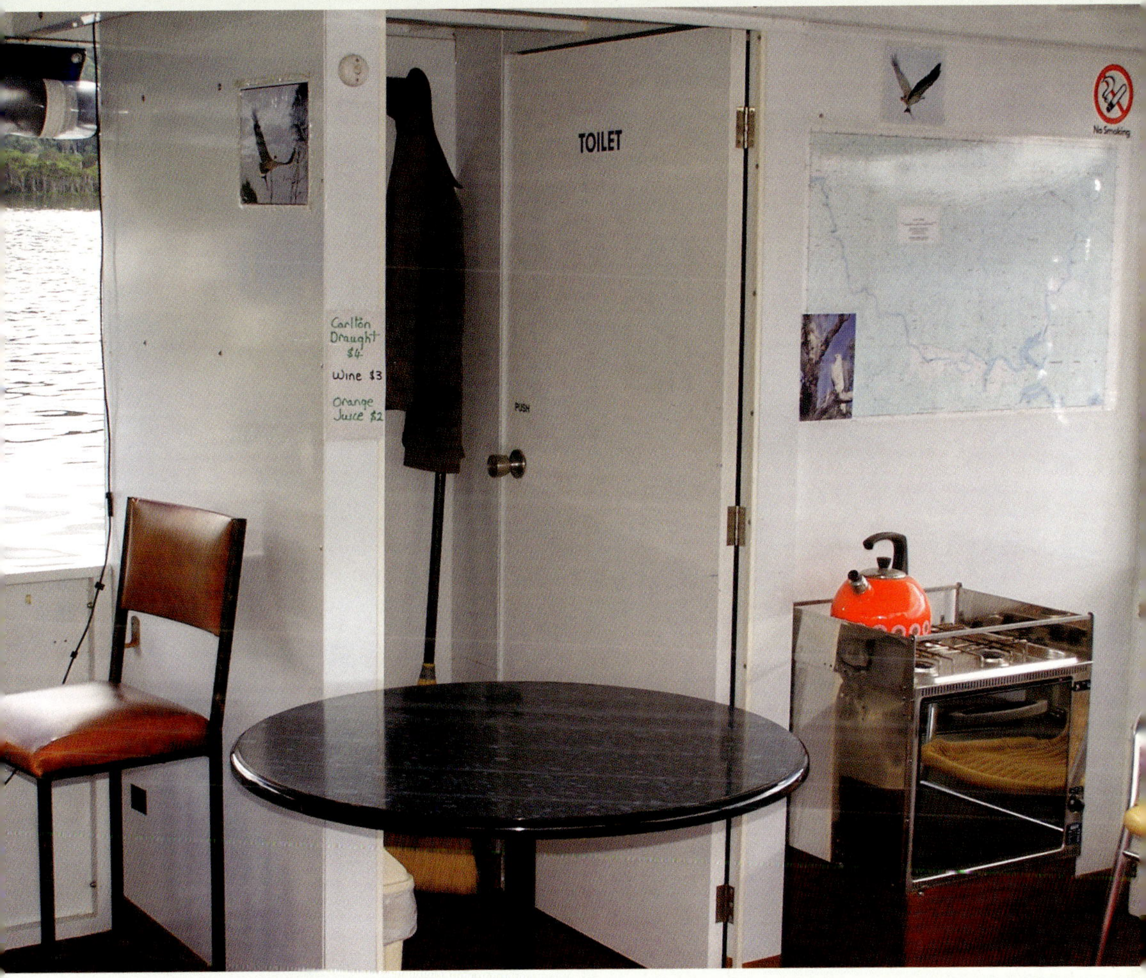

Australia—Gipsy Point, VIC

Wilderness River cruise boat on the Genoa River in north-east Victoria. The highlights of this tour are the bird-spotting possibilities on Maramingo Creek.

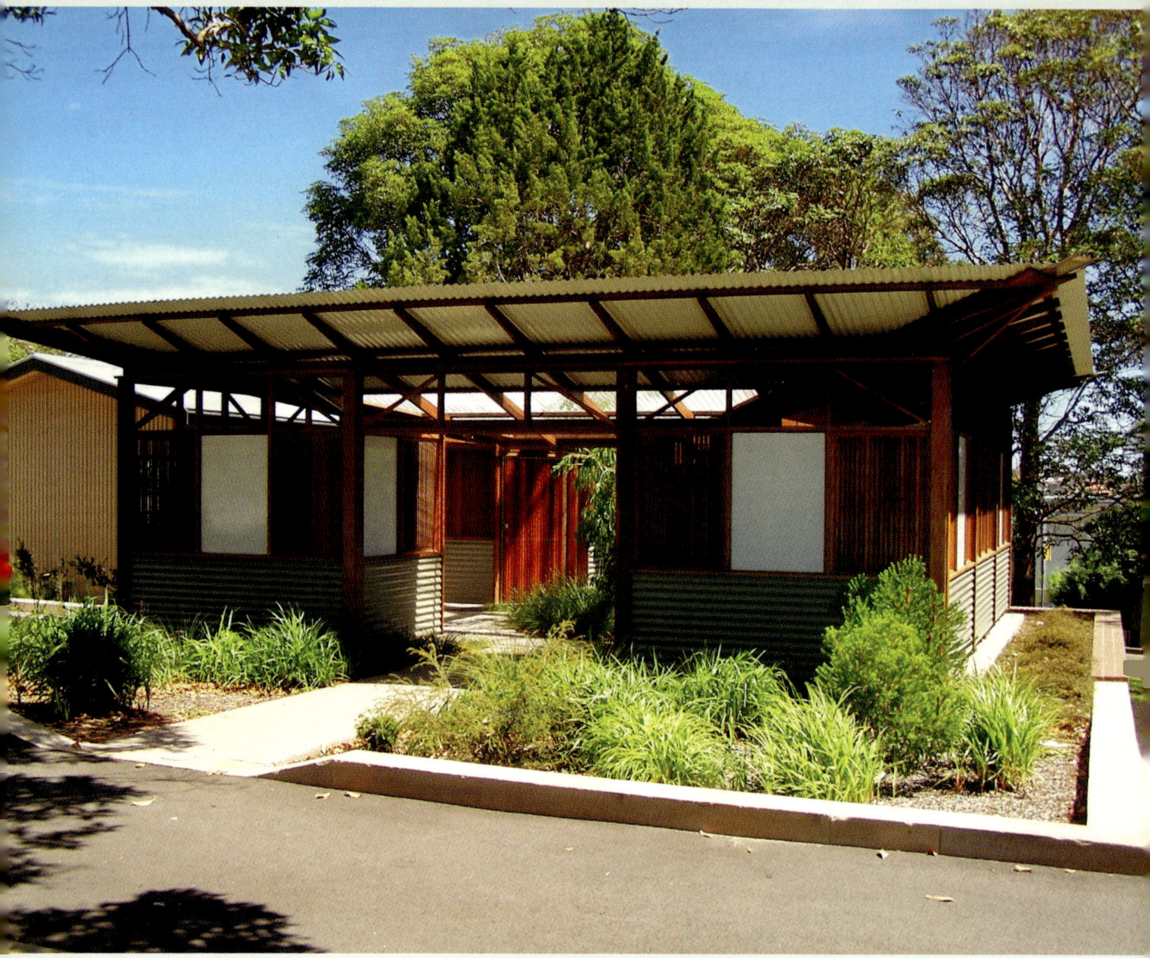

Australia—Mosman, NSW

One of the prettiest designed dunnies in Sydney, complete with an indoor garden and just metres from a beautiful view across Sydney Harbour.

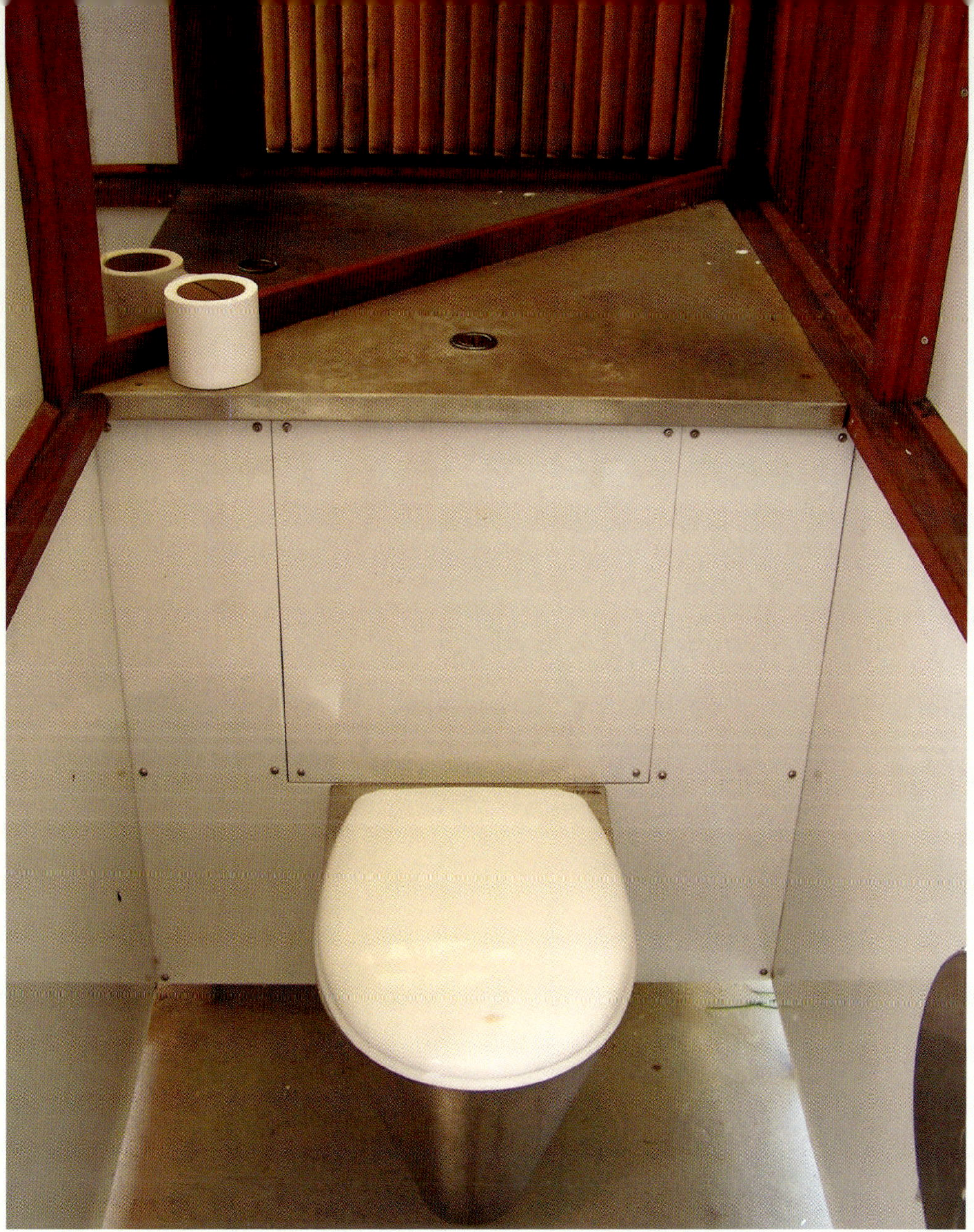

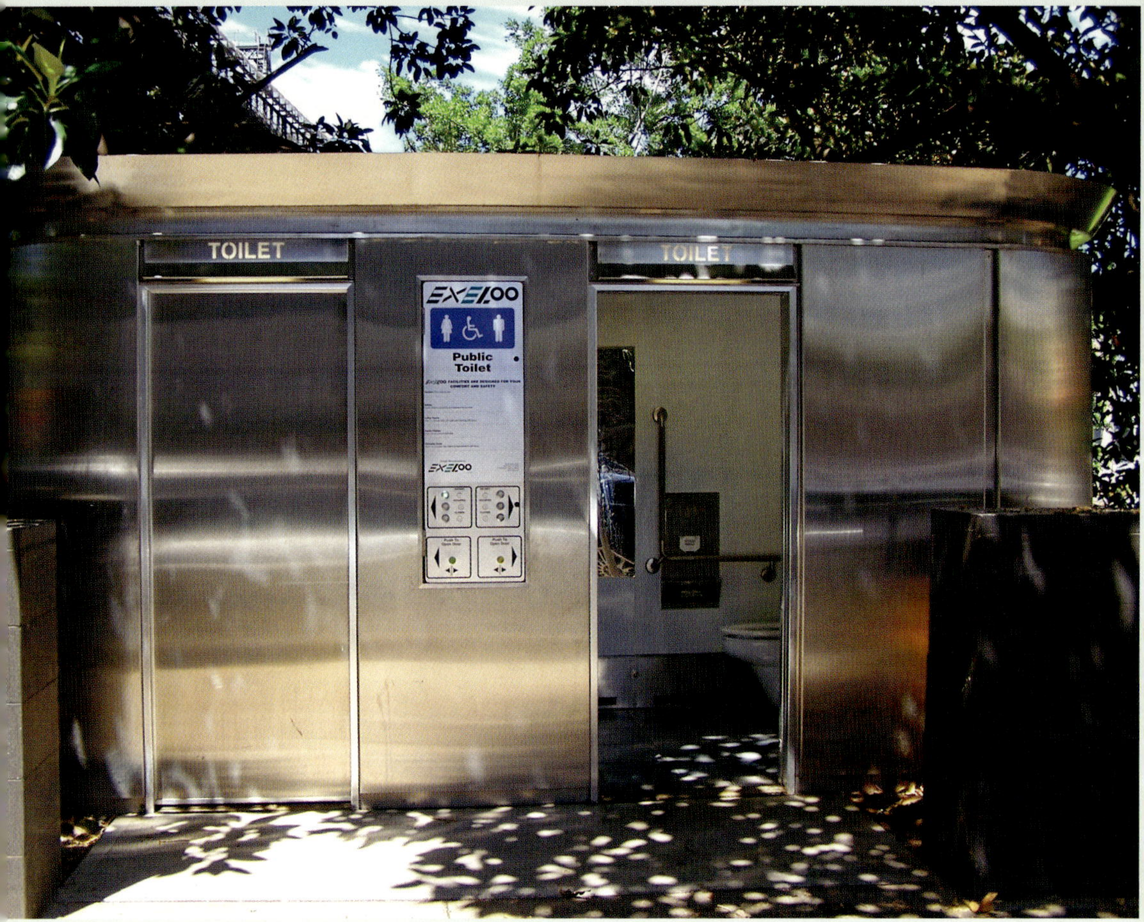

Australia—Kirribilli, NSW
The modern stainless steel variety of public toilet, complete with automatic doors. This one is situated near Luna Park under the Sydney Harbour Bridge.

Australia—Loftus Street, NSW

Years ago in the Sydney CBD, entrances off footpaths to underground dunnies were commonplace. Not so any more. Note the new sandstone where the entrance used to be.

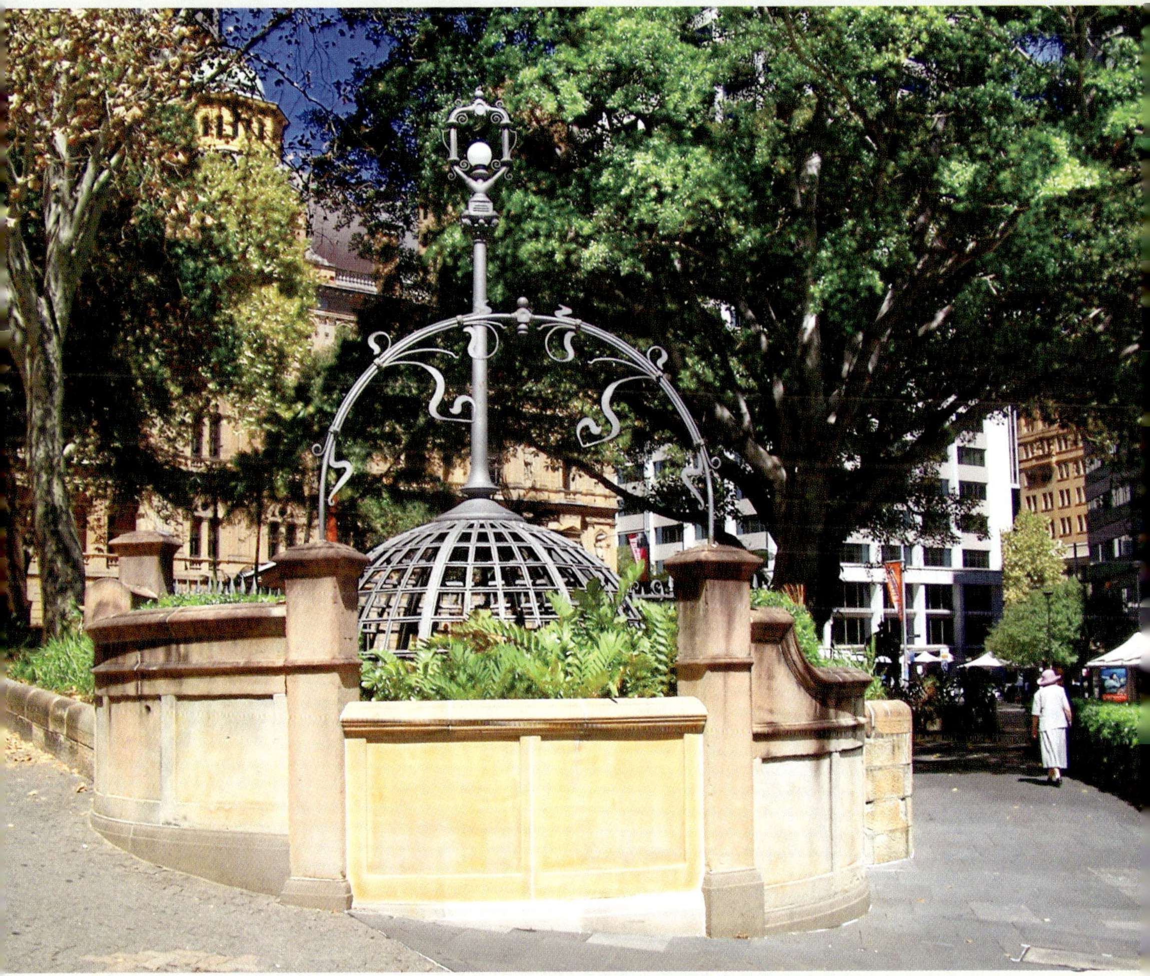

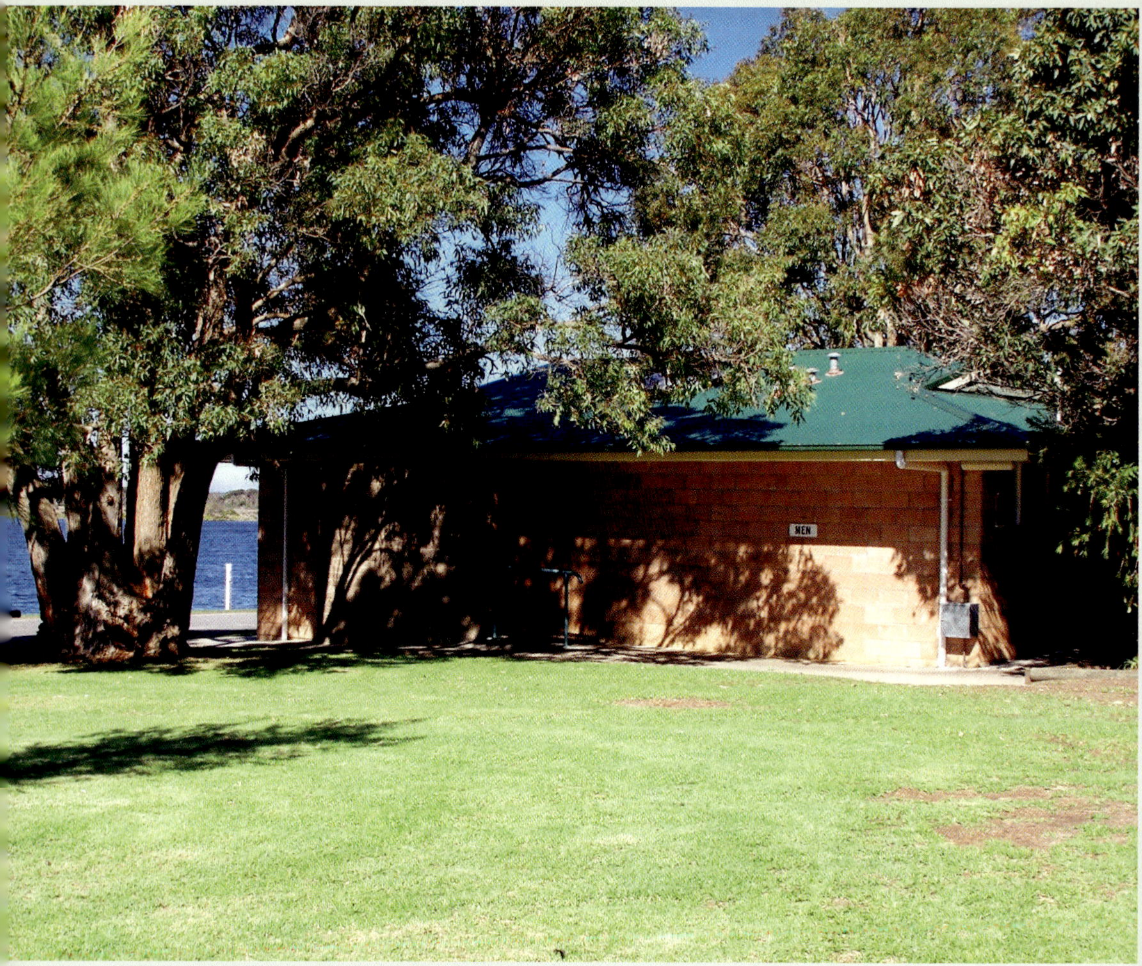

Australia—Mallacoota, VIC

Billed as one of Victoria's best kept secrets, the township of Mallacoota and the surrounding waterways are splendid for fishing, sailing, canoeing and surfing.

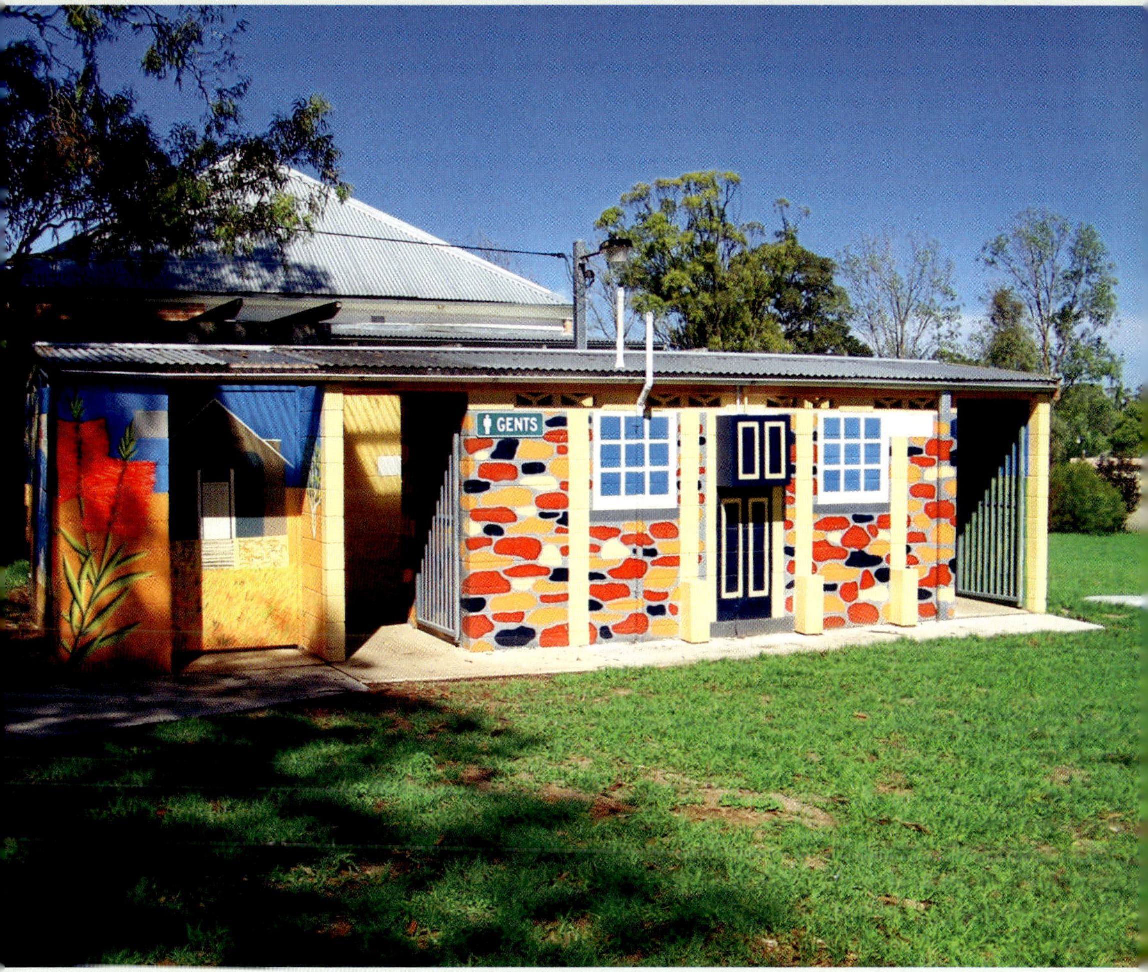

Australia—Marulan, NSW

Marulan is the only town in the world on the 150th meridian, a place where the sun rises at 6 am and sets at 6 pm precisely every equinox.

Australia—Palm Beach, NSW

On or around Australia Day every year for nearly 20 years, 'The Big Swim' has taken place from Palm Beach to Whale Beach. Behind the competitors are the Palm Beach change rooms and toilets. Now a heritage-listed building it was renovated to its former glory some years ago.

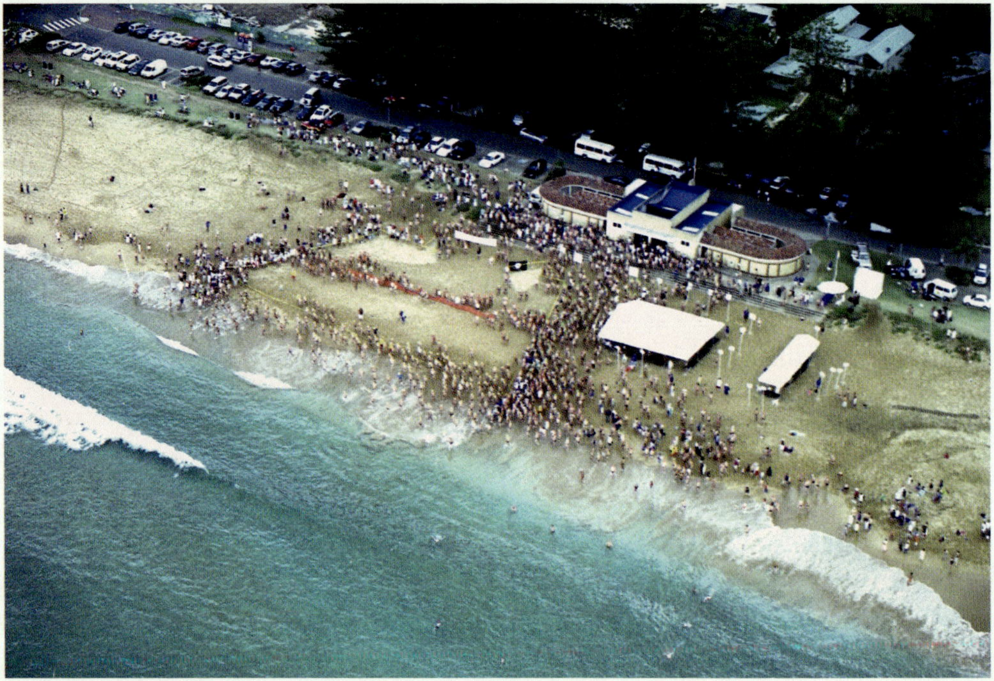

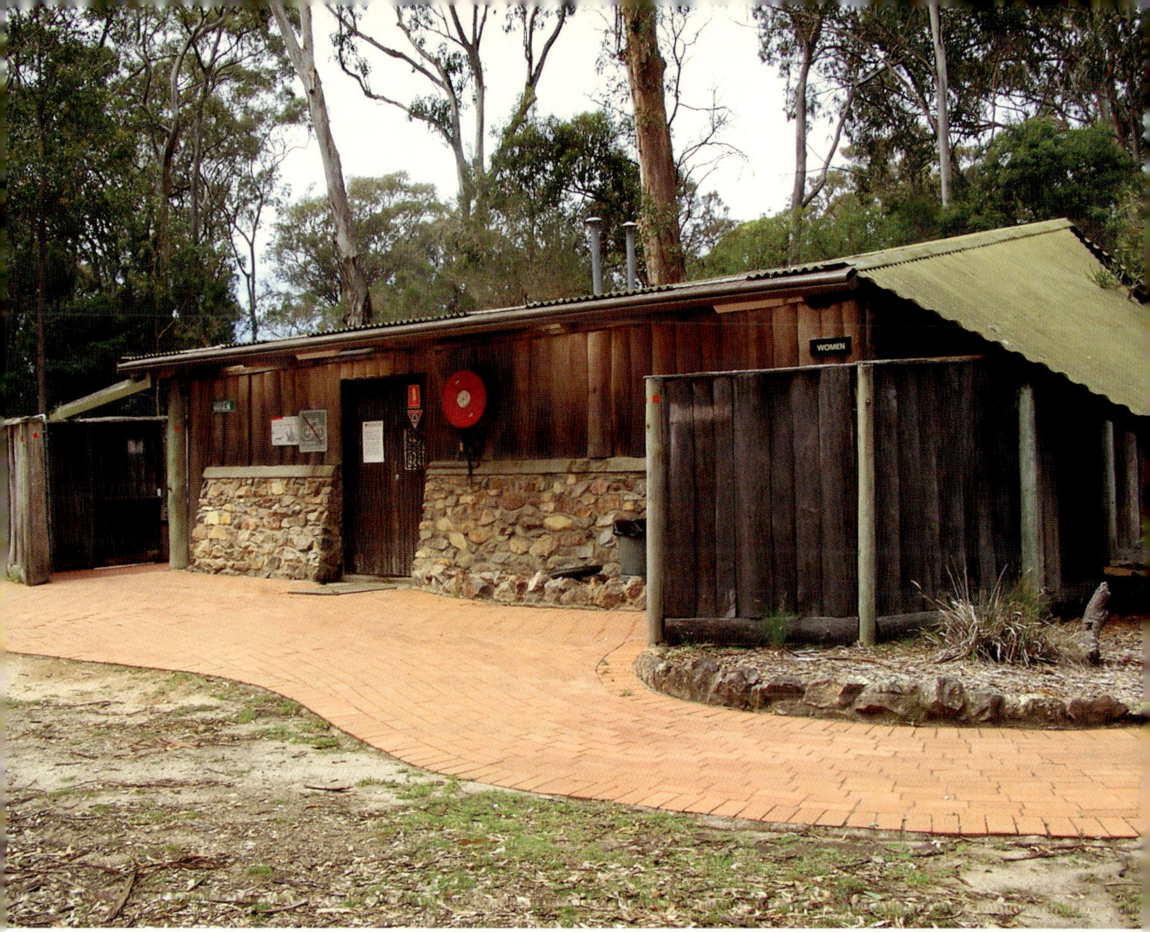

Australia—national park, southern NSW

These days, national parks are a wonderful choice for a true camping experience. Most allow the camper to do a bit of genuine Aussie 'roughing it'. This one, however, had flush toilets and a washing machine.

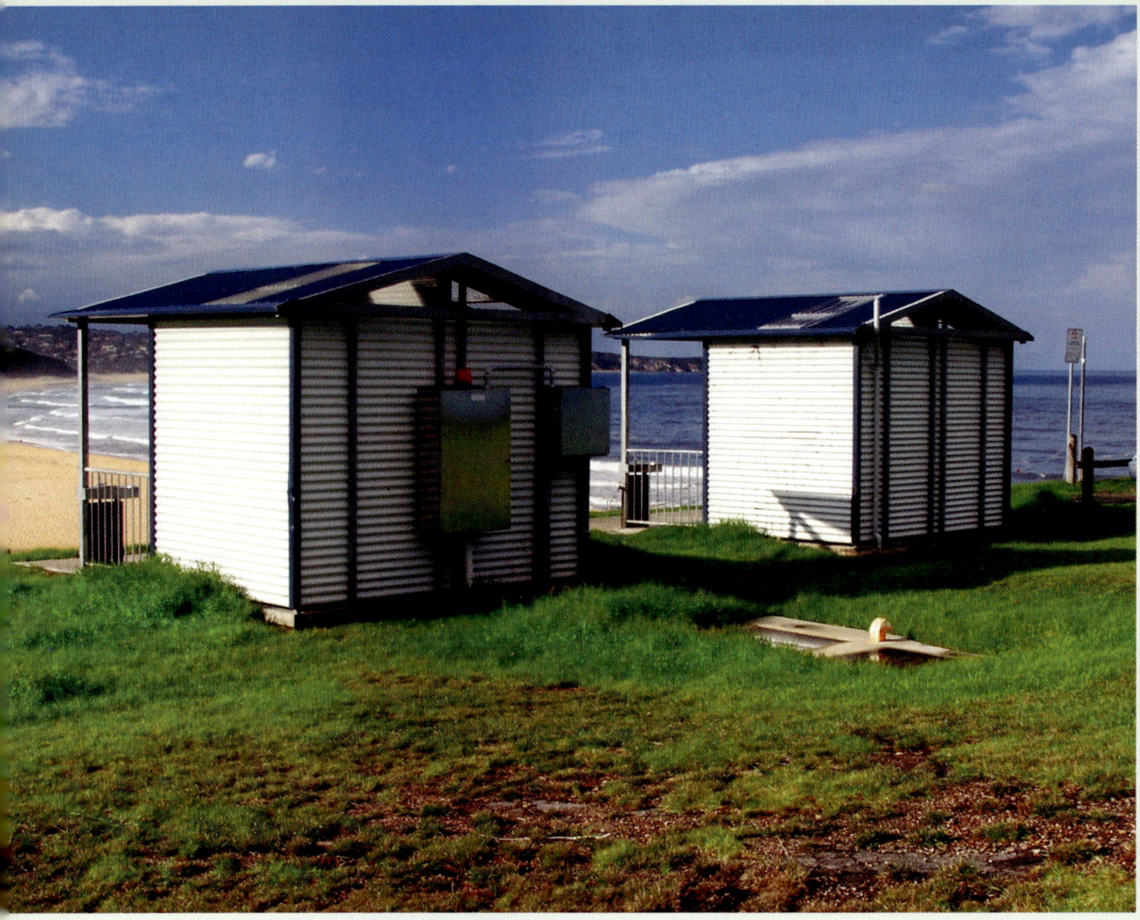

Australia—Merimbula

Known by surfers for its constant little right-hander, Short Point outside Merimbula on the NSW south coast also boasts a magnificent northerly view from the ladies' and gents' toilets.

Australia—South Pambula, NSW

Customer toilets in the local garden centre or nursery.

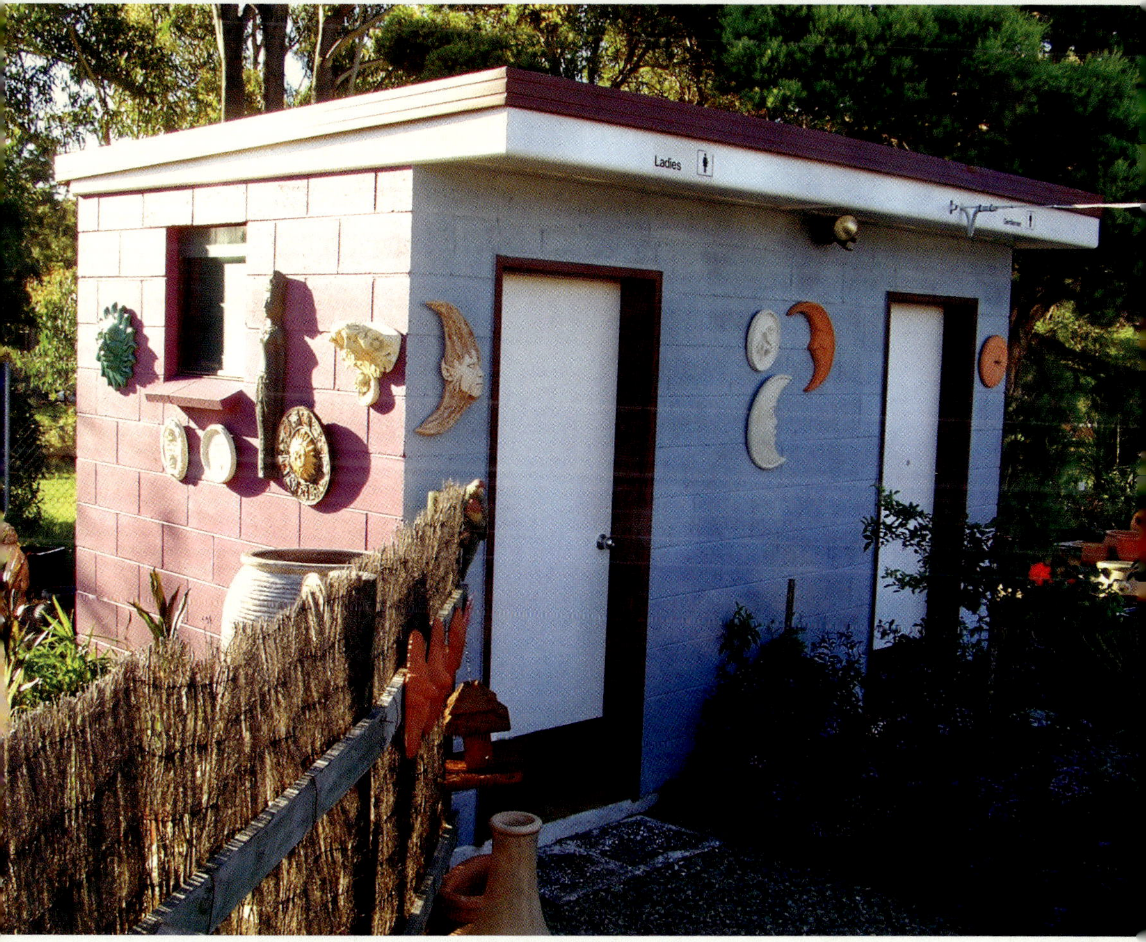

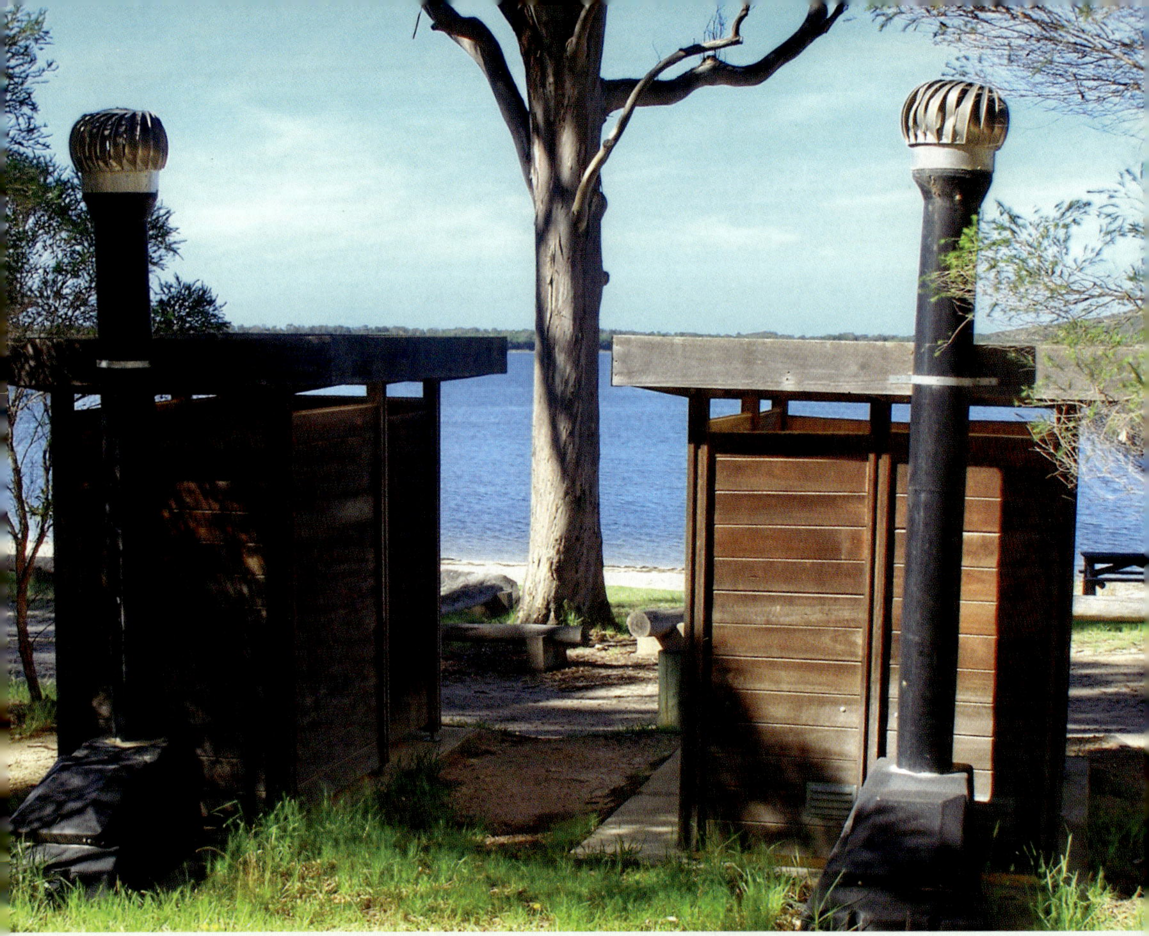

Australia—Wallagoot Lake, NSW

These dunnies service the Wallagoot Lake Sailing Club and the Bournda National Park. The area boasts an array of pristine coastal wilderness. Apart from prolific bird life, dolphin and whale spotting is a common activity.

Australia—Wirriwin Rest Area, NSW

Contemporary style highway toilets ten minutes south of Wollongong. In some parts of the world you have to pay for the privilege of using a roadside toilet. Not in Australia! The road safety authorities realise that people are more likely to stop and therefore rest if there's no charge.

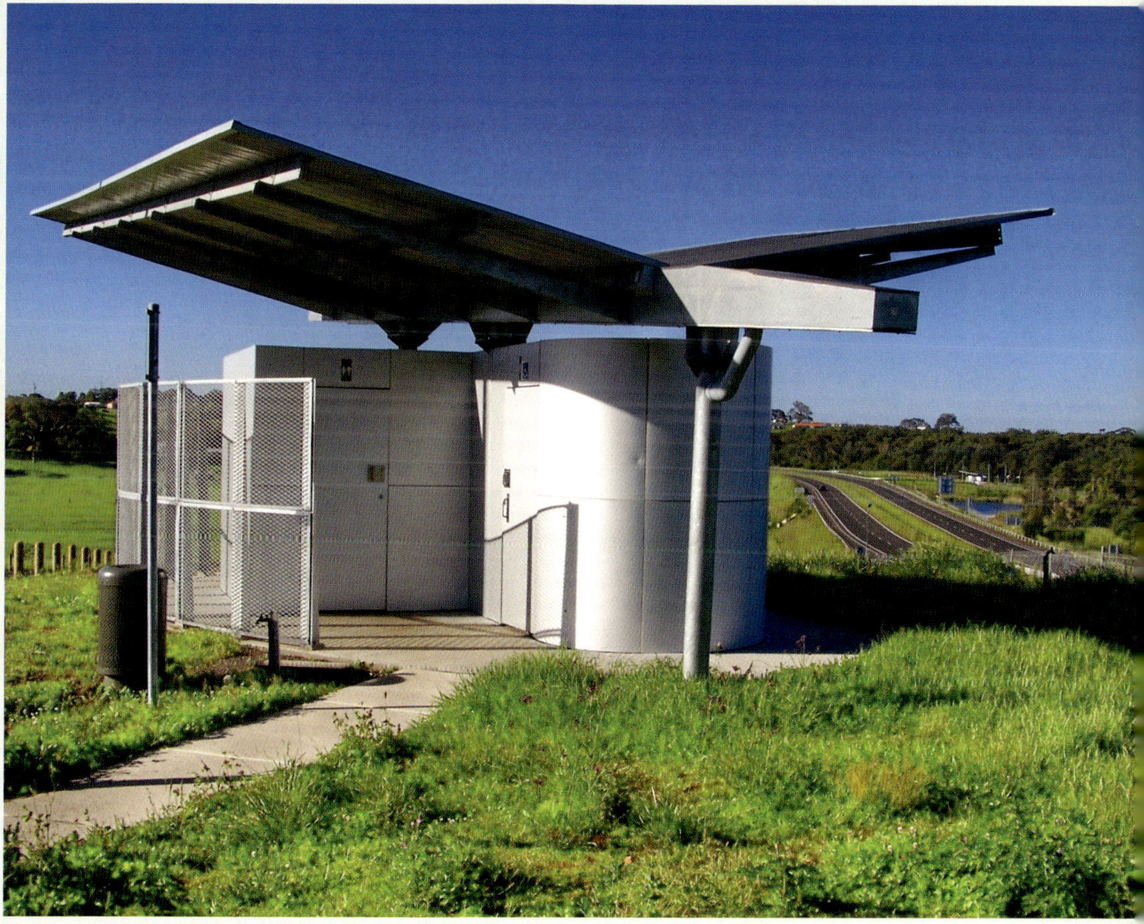

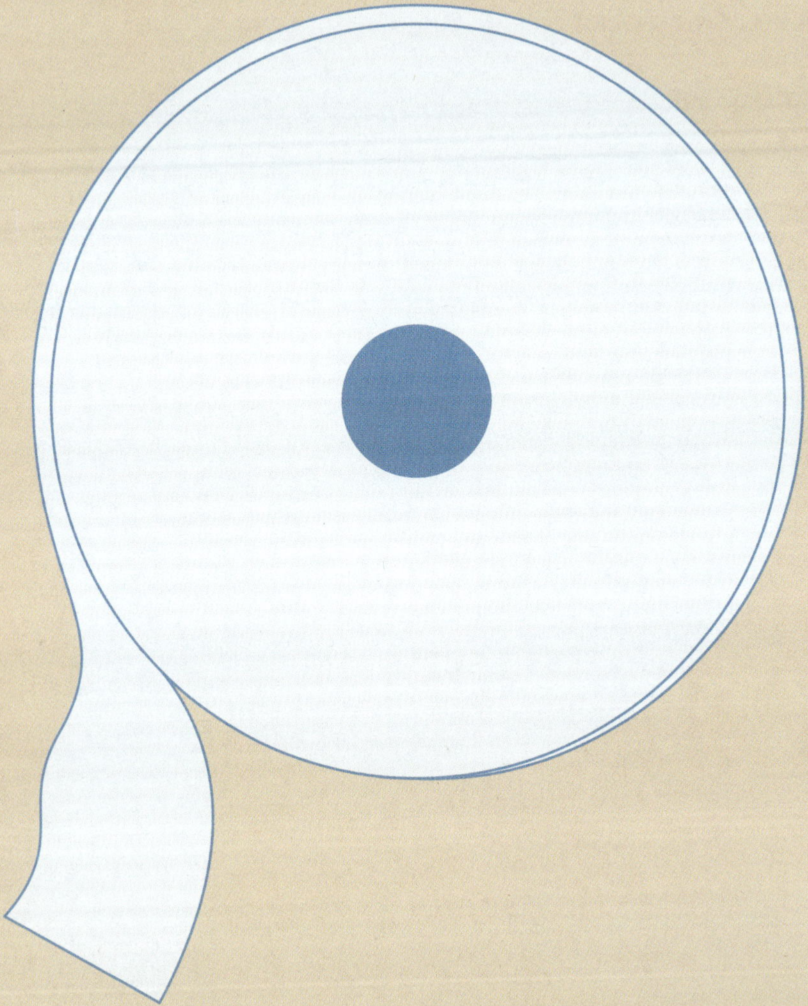

GEOF PRIGGE

Geof Prigge began photographing as a hobby whilst living in Africa in the 1970s. Journeys throughout Europe, Asia, the Americas and the Pacific followed, and actually he was outside Australia more during his twenties than he was at home. He studied journalism, contributing to various environmental and sporting publications over the years, and has had a book published titled *Laugh to Survive*, on the life of Auschwitz survivor Regina Sprada. In 1996 and again in 2001, Geof was commissioned to take photos for a major publishing house. This saw him in China and also Europe on two occasions. After 12 years on Sydney's northern beaches specialising in aerial photography of the east Australian coast, he is again travelling the world working on various photographic assignments which so far have taken him to countries as varied as Nepal, Tibet, India, Greece and the continents of Africa and South America. His sporting passions are sailing and snow skiing. He spent much of 2006 building a school in The Gambia which has included not only school buildings, but a kitchen, library, craft-room and so on, as well as a farm, football field and outside playing area. Toward the end of 2006, he began the process of registering a charity called GLOBAL HANDS—a hands-on Charity Network to promote educational involvement in the third world. Visit www.globalhandscharity.com for more details. His projects are predominantly in West Africa and Nepal.

First published in Australia
in 2007 by
New Holland Publishers (Australia) Pty Ltd
Sydney • Auckland • London • Cape Town

1/66 Gibbes Street Chatswood NSW 2067 Australia
218 Lake Road Northcote Auckland New Zealand
86 Edgware Road London W2 2EA United Kingdom
80 McKenzie Street Cape Town 8001 South Africa

National Library of Australia Cataloguing-in-Publication Data:

Prigge, Geof.
Toilets of the world.

ISBN 9781741105896 (pbk.).

1. Toilets—Pictorial works—Humor. 2. Outhouses—
Pictorial works—Humor. I. Title.

696.182

Publisher: Martin Ford
Designer: Natasha Hayles
Production Manager: Linda Bottari
Production: Liz Malcolm
Printer: Power Printing

10 9 8 7 6 5 4 3 2 1